What People Are Saying . . .

"Sleepy Planet gave us the skills, reassurance, and confidence we needed to make the dream of sleep a fast reality. This approach was truly amazing in helping our family to thrive and we are eternally grateful!"

—Ben Stiller and Christine Taylor, Actors

"Sleepy Planet gave us all the tools we needed to get our baby sleeping through the night. Now when we say goodnight to our daughter, we know it really will be a good night."

—Greg Kinnear, Actor

"With their gentle approach, Sleepy Planet gave us the tools we needed to solve our daughter's sleep problems."

—Liza O'Brien and Conan O'Brien, Television Host

"Sleepy Planet's program is truly miraculous. I now have a baby who is peaceful, rested and happy. It's the answer to every mother's prayer!"

—Julie Moran, Former Host, *Entertainment Tonight*

"While most sleep books just address the how-to's, *The Sleepeasy Solution* speaks directly to the soft-hearted parent who will find great relief in knowing that this approach is well thought out and emotionally sensitive to the entire family."

—Amy Brenneman, Actor

"My baby's well-being means everything to me, and Sleepy Planet not only helped her sleep but put my heart at ease. Our peaceful nights are a huge gift for us all."

—Carnie Wilson, Singer

"Thanks to Sleepy Planet for the advice and kind support. My daughter goes to sleep smiling—what higher praise can I give?"

—Jennifer Beals, Actor

"Sleepy Planet has unparalleled success in giving my families a good night's sleep and provides them with the skills for ongoing, long-term success."

—Alisa Bromberg, M.D., Pediatrician

"I find Sleepy Planet's techniques practical, supportive, nurturing and well reasoned. These methods are wonderfully structured and developmentally sound."

—Stacy L. Waneka, M.D.

"Jennifer and Jill deserve crowns, as they are true sleep royalty."

—Bess Raker, M.D., Pediatrician
Attending Physician, Cedars Sinai Medical Center

"Sleepy Planet has significantly touched the lives of countless families at our center over the past decade."

—Corky Harvey and Wendy Haldeman
Lactation Consultants and Cofounders, The Pump Station

"Because a child's health (and a parent's sanity and patience) is at risk when he is sleep deprived, helping him get a good night's sleep is one of the most important things a parent can do. Sleepy Planet's time-honored solutions ensure that parents have the right information *and* know how to lovingly support their child as he learns to find his path to consistent sleep. Jennifer and Jill's methods succeed where many others fail. So many parents and children in my practice sleep tight thanks to Sleepy Planet! Many thanks to you both!"

—JJ Levenstein, M.D., FAAP
President/Founder, MD Moms, makers of Baby Silk

"With compassion and expertise, Sleepy Planet targets your child's specific sleep needs and supports parents through the emotional side of sleep learning. I highly recommend these methods as both a pediatrician and a mother."

—Sonia Gohill, M.D., Pediatrician

"If you are the parent of a baby or young child and you ever want to get a good night's sleep again, you must read this book! *The Sleepeasy Solution* offers clear solutions and practical advice even the most sleep-deprived parent can benefit from."

—Jane Buckingham, Author, *Modern Girl's Guide to Motherhood*

"Sleepy Planet gives tired parents simple techniques and gentle support that help them to resolve their child's sleep problems within days! This book is a must-read for all parents with young children."

—Peter Waldstein, M.D., Pediatrician

"As a pediatrician, I frequently see parents in my practice who are baffled about how to resolve their child's sleep problems. I often refer them to Sleepy Planet because I know they will be guided and supported sensitively through the difficult process of helping their child learn to sleep."

—Sheila Phillips, M.D., Pediatrician

"This book offers parents techniques that work fast and loads of support around the emotional side of sleep learning. With these essential tools, the whole family will be sleeping in no time."

—Dr. Jenn Berman, Author, *The A-Z Guide to Raising Happy, Confident Kids*

"Now my daughter is going to bed with a smile. This approach is miraculous!"

—Bonnie Z., Mother

"Just wanted to let you know that Logan has been sleeping beautifully since we last spoke! Two nights ago, he slept from 7:30 PM until 6:30 AM without waking once! It was like we'd gone to sleep heaven! I feel like I'm on happy pills! I can't thank you enough for your assistance. We are deeply grateful!"

—Jana R., mother of 6-month-old Logan

"Oliver just went to sleep tonight after two minutes and I am ecstatic. I feel like the shackles of bedtime have been removed, and I am myself again. I couldn't have done it without your support and reassuring belief that Oliver could and would sleep on his own. Thank you so much. You're the best."

—Jessica Y., mother of 14-month-old Oliver

"My husband and I were in a serious state of depression and anxiety due to the fact that our baby girl, Annabelle, was not sleeping. Annabelle was also in quite a state—cranky and irritable—due to only getting 8–9 hours of sleep a day. With your support and guidance, we were able to stick with the sleep training process and be consistent with Annabelle. She is now a terrific sleeper. At 11½ months, Annabelle is the happiest baby I know. She smiles all the time, laughs out loud and loves to be around people. She sleeps 11 to 12 hours at night and takes 2 regular naps a day. We know for sure that Annabelle is growing well and enjoying life because she is 'well slept.' Thank you, thank you, thank you!"

—Melanie D., mother of 11½-month-old Annabelle

the sleepeasy solution

The Exhausted Parent's Guide to Getting Your Child to Sleep —from Birth to Age 5

Jennifer Waldburger, LCSW, and **Jill Spivack,** LMSW
Cofounders of Sleepy Planet—Helping the World Sleep, One Child at a Time

Health Communications, Inc.
Deerfield Beach, Florida

www.hcibooks.com

This book contains advice and information related to sleep for children from birth through five years. It is not intended to substitute for medical or developmental advice. Consult your pediatrician and/or lactation consultant before beginning any sleep program to verify that your plan is acceptable for your particular child.

Library of Congress Cataloging-in-Publication Data

Waldburger, Jennifer.
The sleepeasy solution : the exhausted parent's guide to getting your child to sleep—from birth to age five / Jennifer Waldburger, Jill Spivack.
    p. cm.
    Includes bibliographical references and index.
ISBN-13: 978-0-7573-0560-3 (trade paper : alk. paper)
ISBN-10: 0-7573-0560-1 (trade paper : alk. paper)
    1. Children—Sleep.   2. Child rearing.   I. Spivack, Jill.   II. Title
    BF723.S45W35 2007
    649'.6—dc22

                                        2006039373

Publisher: Health Communications, Inc.
           3201 S.W. 15th Street
           Deerfield Beach, FL 33442-8190

R-10-08

Cover design by Andrea Perrine Brower
Interior book design by Lawna Patterson Oldfield
Additional cover layout and typography by Adam Gordon

CONTENTS

Foreword ix

Acknowledgments xi

Introduction: We Feel Your Pain xv

CHAPTER ONE:
You Don't Have to Live Like This!..1

CHAPTER TWO:
Creating Your Child's Custom Sleep Plan............................11

*Sleep Stealer #1: No Consistent Bedtime Routine • Sleep Stealer #2: Your
Child Needs You to Fall Asleep • Sleep Stealer #3: Poor Sleep
Environment • Sleep Stealer #4: Misusing Sleep Aids • Sleep Stealer #5:
Mistimed Sleep Schedule • Sleep Stealer #6: Limit Testing • Sleep
Stealer #7: Night Noshing*

CHAPTER THREE:
Step-by-Step Sleep...53

CHAPTER FOUR:
The Truth About Crying: Supporting Your Child While He
Learns to Sleep...75

CHAPTER FIVE:
The Art of the Nap...85

CHAPTER SIX:

Alternative Methods for Sleep Learning 111

CHAPTER SEVEN:

Developmental Issues and How They Affect Sleep: Birth to Twelve Months 123

Separation Anxiety (Birth to 9 Months) • Teething • Starting Solids • Hitting a Developmental Milestone • Separation Anxiety (9 to 12 Months)

CHAPTER EIGHT:

Developmental Issues and How They Affect Sleep: Twelve to Twenty-Four Months 151

Busy, Busy, Busy! • Separation Anxiety (12 to 18 Months) • Language Burst • Separation Anxiety (18 to 24 Months) • Resistance to Napping or Bedtime • Potty Training

CHAPTER NINE:

Developmental Issues and How They Affect Sleep: Two to Five Years 173

Fears • Nightmares • Night Terrors • Separation Anxiety • Anxiety About Starting School • The Birth of a New Sibling • Potty Training

CHAPTER TEN:

Special Situations 203

Conclusion: From Our Hearts to Yours 245

Appendix A: Your Custom Sleep Planners 247

Appendix B: Crying 911 (Emergency Help for Panicked Parents)...259

Appendix C: Sleep Chart 267

Appendix D: Average Sleep Needs by Age 269

Resources 271

References 277

Index 279

FOREWORD

I f you are like most parents, you truly—and rightfully—panic at the prospect of teaching your child how to sleep through the night. It's easy to picture a worst-case scenario in which your child is crying as you stand by feeling helpless and guilty. As a result, many parents rationalize bad sleep habits, coming up with excuses for why their children must be rocked to sleep or eat throughout the night.

But what we tend to forget is that children—just like their parents—really do want to sleep through the night. The difference is that we already know how; our children have to learn. So how do you teach your child to sleep in a way that doesn't break your heart and that ensures healthy sleep habits for a lifetime? Can it be done without having your child "scream it out"?

As a pediatrician and the mother of two young children, I know all too well about the struggles with sleep. In my own home, despite the advice I give all day long about letting a baby learn to self-soothe, I experienced firsthand how easy it is to doubt yourself in the middle of the night. When each of my children cried, I wanted to hold and console them, even though I knew that "helping" them didn't actually help them sleep. The challenge is to find a balance. On the one hand, you must help your child learn the essential skills he or she needs to self-soothe. On the other hand, you must support your helpless baby or limit-testing toddler with love and affection. Finding this balance is where most parents get lost.

Jill Spivack and Jennifer Waldburger are exceptionally good at guiding parents out of the sleep-learning maze. They give their advice with full hearts, knowing the struggles you face when the sun goes down and it is time for your child to go to bed. They've helped many of my own patients get through the sleep-learning process quickly, with minimal tears. In this book, they offer the same essential tools that they use in their private practice. The most important aspect of teaching good sleep habits is to have a solid plan of action, so you'll know what to do in the middle of the night when your defenses are down and your resolve is tested. In these moments, and throughout the sleep-learning process, this book will be the most important item on your nightstand.

Research shows that our health is intimately tied to the quality of our rest. Kids grow when they sleep. They wake up happier, more active, and less moody when they sleep well and for long stretches. As parents, we all know that we are more patient and more capable of enjoying time with our children when we are well rested. Sleep is not a luxury; it is a necessity. For parents and children, the quality of our sleep is as important as the quality of the air we breathe and the food we eat. Jennifer and Jill will ensure that you finally begin to get the rest so essential to your entire family's well-being.

Cara Natterson, M.D.
Pediatrician and author of
Your Newborn: Head to Toe and
Your Toddler: Head to Toe

ACKNOWLEDGMENTS

Jennifer would like to thank . . .

My amazing family, Anne, Richard, Stefanie, and Erica, for your understanding and patience while I disappeared during the writing of this book. Your unwavering faith in all of my endeavors never ceases to amaze me, and I am so grateful for your incredible support.

Derek and Linda O'Neill, all the "lads and lasses," and my Ireland family, for bringing so much love and light to my life. Whenever I leap, you are the net that appears.

The Prema Agni Foundation, for teaching me about what really matters.

Lois Thompson, Liora Elghanayan, Nicole Cornthwaite, Sherri Greene, Jodie Rufty, Stephanie Azaria, Phylliss Del Greco, Kathy Mulligan, Elise Lane, David Rogers, Claire Luft, Brook Still, Erin Patterson, John Seibert, Ginger Christie, Mitch and Hank Cohen, Cynthia True, Tara Nalepinski, Laura Darke, and Laurie Eisenberg, for your inspiration and encouragement.

Jill Spivack, my business partner and lifelong friend, for showing up at the rental office needing a college roommate, for having a baby who didn't sleep, and for inspiring me always to reach higher and dig deeper. Watching our dreams unfold together has been one of my greatest joys.

Jill would like to thank . . .

My husband, Gary, for giving me roots to ground me and wings to fly. Without your love and commitment to our family and tremendous patience, I could have never followed my dreams.

My children, Jake and Emma, whose simple existence has inspired me in countless ways and has contributed to a better understanding of myself both as a mother and as a professional.

Jennifer Waldburger, my soul sister and colleague. Your endless emotional support and dedication to our friendship and work relationship have given me the courage to forge ahead both personally and professionally for the past twenty years.

My father, Stan Lassoff, who has lent me his lifelong support, given me his weekly words of wisdom, instilled in me a commitment to others, and has never allowed me to lose faith in myself.

My mother, Joan Eisenberg, for always believing in me and imparting to me the guidance that women should have their own career but prioritize their families above all else.

My in-laws, Doris and John Spivack, who have been incredibly understanding throughout this process and have cooked many a dinner for my family when I was unavailable.

Natalie Weinstein, for being a terrific friend and support and for all of her brainstorming sessions on the title of this book.

My dog, Otto, who missed many walks and hikes to allow me to complete this project and still loved me anyway.

Jill and Jennifer would like to thank . . .

All of the moms, dads, babies, and children we have worked with over the years, who have taught us at least as much as we have taught them.

Julie Carson May, for her expert guidance and wisdom—and for believing in us before we did.

Allison Janse, for her excellent editorial support and creative ideas, and everyone at HCI for their enthusiasm for this project.

Mary Lengle and Paola Fernandez, for helping to get the word out.

Corky Harvey, Wendy Haldeman, Carol Patton, and everyone at the Pump Station for their expertise and generous support.

Adam Gordon, Alisa Fishbach, David Altschuler, Rachel O'Brien, and Roxana Kennedy, whose hard work and dedication we appreciate more than you'll ever know.

Rachel Klauber-Speiden, Melanie Praeger, Michael Levin, and all of our clients, friends, and loved ones whose input and assistance helped to shape this book and bring it out into the world.

Before you became a parent, your experiences with sleepless nights were probably few and far between. Sure, every so often you had the flu and were up all night, but you were able to take the day off work and recover. Or maybe you had occasional late nights out with your spouse or friends, talking and laughing till the wee hours. You may have wondered what all of the fuss was with your sleep-deprived friends who had children, secretly thinking, "Why can't they just put their kid to sleep? How hard is it to get a baby down for bed?" (And while you were at it, you may have imagined that your girlfriends with babies who "didn't work" had hours free to lounge around drinking lattes.)

Flash forward to the present day: Now you're the parent. We're venturing to guess, if you've purchased this book, that you may feel as if the karma police have paid you back big time by giving you your own child with a sleep problem. Welcome to the club! But don't worry; your doubts about your friends' intelligence did not curse you into having a sleep fighter forever, and besides, you're in very good company. Sleep—or lack thereof—is perhaps the most frequently discussed topic among parents of children from birth to five years old. Everyone talks about sleep, but this precious commodity is in dangerously short supply in far too many households. Our recognition of this crisis is what led us to open our sleep-consulting practice, Sleepy Planet—and although we've now helped thousands of families throughout the country and across the globe get the rest they so desperately need, there are many thousands more who are still struggling. Chances are that if you bought this book, then you are one of those families, and our hearts go out to you.

We have the deepest empathy for what it feels like to stand in your shoes. You are so tired you can't think straight or function, and you can't even remember when you and your spouse last had a date night. But you love your child madly and would do anything to make sure she knows it—including feeding or rocking her to sleep, lying down with her in bed, or rushing to her side whenever she cries at night. You are a loving, caring parent who just wants what's best for your child.

And yet your child is not sleeping well, and that's wreaking havoc on your whole family. Desperate for answers, you may have read other books, talked to anyone who will listen, and scoured the Internet for solutions. But somehow, maddeningly, your sleep problems remain unresolved. We hope you know that your child's sleep problems do not stem from a lack of intelligence on your part. The families who come to see us at Sleepy Planet are bright, educated people who pride themselves on making informed decisions about their children. We've seen mothers and fathers with more degrees than we can count on one hand—doctors, lawyers, researchers, and business executives—who have felt miserably lost about how to resolve their child's night wakings or nap problems. The dedicated parents who come to see us for help have tried just about anything, including sleeping in the bed (or even the crib) with their child, to get a good night's sleep. Many even already know what their "bad habits" are, or at least some of what they need to do differently. So if they're so smart—if *you're* so smart—then why aren't you all getting some serious shut-eye?

The answer is simple: when it comes to your child, there's emotion involved; you love him more than anything, and your brain can't ignore what your heart is guiding you to do. When it's 3:00 AM and your child isn't sleeping, your *head* might tell you that spending hours rocking or walking with him, or pulling him into bed, isn't an ideal solution, but your *heart* is insisting that he's crying, he's upset, and you must help him. So what's a loving, intelligent parent to do?

Our goal at Sleepy Planet has always been to encourage parents to listen to their own natural instincts while providing them with the information they need to resolve their sleep problems quickly. Drawing from the current available research on children and sleep, our backgrounds in child development and psychotherapy, and hands-on parenting, we also offer years of experience in having helped thousands of families through the sleep-learning process. But arguably the most important element to our approach is the one that also ensures our families' success: we carefully address the *emotional* aspects of teaching your child to sleep, so your child continues to feel loved and supported, and so *you* feel supported, too. In our experience, finding a happy medium between head and heart is the best way to help a child sleep better, because it doesn't force parents into the extremes of either cold, clinical efficiency ("He's gotta sleep, so he's gotta cry it out alone") or completely ignoring the family's need for sleep ("Who cares if we're all exhausted and miserable? We'll just keep holding him because he's crying!"). It's this critical balance that gives parents the confidence to know that they're doing what's best for their children—and that helps families sleep well *fast*.

"No-Cry" Versus "Crying It Out"

Most parents wanting to make changes with their child's sleep have heard all the debates about allowing a child to cry. This has led to a lot of confusion. Some of the methods that promise "no-cry" solutions suggest to parents that their child won't ever cry. The idea is that being "gentler and more responsive"—continuing to soothe your child by patting, picking her up, holding her hand, and the like—means that she is less traumatized. Ironically, though, parents often report that the child still cries even while they continue to attend to her; all children protest change, and the way they let us know they don't like the change is to cry. As important as it is for parents to express love to children through physical touch, and as illogical as it may seem that doing so while helping a child learn to sleep is counterproductive, it is indeed the parent's touch that can exacerbate a child's frustration in this scenario. The result? The child often continues to struggle with sleep, usually for weeks or even months, because she is not being allowed to learn how to soothe *herself*. With older children, using touch can be especially detrimental, as it tempts them to continue testing limits with you, to keep pressing until you cave in and help them to sleep. We've found that when using these kinds of "hands-on" methods, parents often give up on sleep learning because it takes so long to actually get better sleep that the process itself becomes exhausting.

On the other end of the spectrum are the experts who suggest that the fastest way to help a child to sleep is to allow him to "cry it out"—in other words, shutting the door and leaving your child completely alone, crying, for as long as it takes him to fall asleep. Also known as *full extinction*, this method actually does work, and sometimes quite quickly—although we have heard stories of children who have cried for as long as several hours at a stretch on the first night or two, perhaps bewildered and frightened because the usual helpers (namely, you) have disappeared. The idea of a child alone in the dark, crying inconsolably, doesn't sit right with most parents, and it doesn't sit right with us, either. It seems unnecessarily hard on both parents and child.

We think experts on both ends of the spectrum are well intentioned, but we also believe that the so-called no-cry solutions focus too much on the parent's and child's emotions and not enough on the necessary conditions for learning, and that the extinction methods focus too much on the child's learning and not enough on the emotional side of sleep learning. This is how we arrived at what we call the "least-cry" approach.

The "Least-Cry" Approach

So if giving your child *too much* help makes her cry harder and longer, and giving her *too little* help makes parents (and possibly the child) feel uneasy and overwhelmed, what's left? Finding a balance between allowing your child to learn how to sleep, while lovingly supporting her in the process. Our recipe for successful sleep learning—meaning that children learn to sleep quickly with a minimum of crying—contains two important ingredients:

1. A simple, customized sleep plan that includes step-by-step instructions for scheduling, environmental changes, and helping children change their sleep behavior, and

2. Plenty of support around the emotional aspects of teaching a child to sleep (and some inevitable frustration), to help children continue to feel loved, and to help parents remain consistent as their child learns.

Parents who use our methods usually report that their child begins to sleep through the night in less than five nights, because the child receives clear, consistent responses that shape behavior quickly, and because she feels your loving encouragement while she learns. In a matter of days, children learn that they *don't* need assistance from their parents—with a bit of practice they become expert sleepers, and the whole family finally begins to get the rest they need.

Although there are other methods designed to offer parents a "middle-of-the-road" option, we haven't found any that help a child learn as quickly and minimize the crying as effectively as the techniques we use. We believe this is because we offer an *equal* balance of opportunities for behavioral learning and loving support that doesn't interfere with that learning. In this book, our aim is to give you exactly what a family would get if they were sitting in our office: our expertise, proper tools, and all the emotional support you need. We'll help you create an organized, fail-proof plan that ensures success—usually in less than five nights. At Sleepy Planet, we've met thousands of parents who are in exactly the same exhausted, barely functioning boat that you're in right now. Happily, your child's (and thus you and your spouse's) sleepless nights will soon feel like a quickly fading bad dream—so hang in there; help has finally arrived! (That would be us, and we're not leaving your side till your child's sleep is much improved. Promise.)

How to Use This Book

We developed this book with extreme parental exhaustion in mind. We know you want to be sleeping as quickly as possible, so if you'd like to jump-start the process, you can skip right to the how-to chapters: Chapter 2, "Creating Your Child's Custom Sleep Plan" and Chapter 3, "Step-by-Step Sleep." Eventually, though, you'll want to read the other chapters, too, because your understanding of the issues they present will help you stay consistent as you help your child sleep and will speed you through the process.

Chapter 1, "You Don't Have to Live Like This!" will help you understand the vital importance of everyone getting enough rest and the ways in which your child's sleep deprivation can dangerously put his health at risk. In the section entitled "How Sleep Deprivation Affects Your Marriage," you'll learn that although children require constant caregiving, chronic neglect of your own needs as parents is a recipe for family disaster.

Chapters 2 and 3, "Creating Your Child's Custom Sleep Plan" and "Step-by-Step Sleep," contain the "nuts and bolts" information that will speed you on your way toward getting great sleep. Both you and your partner should read these chapters carefully, as you'll want to fully understand the process—and feel in sync with each other—as you begin helping your child learn how to sleep. You'll find your very own Sleep Planners—one for crib sleepers and one for bed sleepers—in Appendix A at the end of the book, allowing you to create a customized sleep plan for your child and family. If you prefer, you can simply jot down your own notes instead of using the planner. In Appendix C, we've included a Sleep Chart to help you track your child's progress.

Chapter 4, "The Truth About Crying: Supporting Your Child While He Learns to Sleep," addresses all of your concerns about your child's well-being as he moves through the sleep-learning process. We understand how torturous it can be for parents when their child cries, and in reality, there is no way for a child to learn how to sleep without *some* frustration. For additional support, we created a special appendix entitled "Crying 911 (Emergency Help for Panicked Parents)." Be sure to put a glow-in-the-dark bookmark in this section of the book, as the information contained here will help you understand exactly how to take care of your child when she cries—and how to take care of your own feelings, too. It will come in especially handy in the middle of the night when you're feeling like you may need some additional words of encouragement.

In Chapter 5, "The Art of the Nap," we'll help you plan your nap schedule based on your child's age and walk you step by step through how to help your child nap better. Although we've made a separate chapter for naps, please note that we encourage parents to work on night sleep and nap sleep at the same time. In other words, you'll begin working on naps the morning after you've completed your first night of sleep learning.

In Chapter 6, "Alternative Methods for Sleep Learning," we offer variations on our techniques for parents who wish to help their child more throughout the learning process. Although children will take longer to learn with more assistance, some parents feel more at ease taking things a bit slower. We also thoroughly address cosleeping in this chapter.

There are three central chapters to further educate you on your child's development and how it affects sleep: Chapter 7, for babies from birth to twelve months; Chapter 8, for toddlers twelve to twenty-four months; and Chapter 9, for children two to five years old. You'll return to these chapters often as your child grows, to troubleshoot any developmental issues affecting his sleep.

Chapter 10, "Special Situations," covers such issues as twins and multiples, colic and reflux, transitioning your child from a crib to a bed, and issues that working and single parents face. For troubleshooting during the sleep-learning process, or if your child's sleep falls off track in the future, be sure to read the section in this chapter entitled "Bumps in the Road." This section offers tips on how to handle developmental milestones, illness, teething, travel, and other situations that may temporarily affect your child's ability to sleep well.

Together, these chapters cover all that you'll need to feel grounded and supported in the decisions you'll make to help your child sleep better.

Thousands of Happy, Rested Families Can't Be Wrong!

What we've learned over years of helping families solve their sleep problems is that when they have the right combination of clear, organized information, plus the warm support of a coach—who helps to manage difficult feelings that arise, reminds them to be consistent, and helps them troubleshoot along the way—they really can't fail. Following in the footsteps of thousands of families before you, now it's your turn to begin to enjoy life again—and to thrive.

So let's get started. You're about to embark on a journey that has immeasurable rewards, and we'll be there with you every step of the way. And just think—a great night's sleep could be just seventy-two hours away.

CHAPTER ONE

You Don't Have to Live Like This!

Before we began working as sleep consultants, we were practicing psychotherapists and parenting-group leaders who worked with lots of children and families. Many of the babies we saw were unusually cranky and fussy, and many of the children were having emotional or behavioral problems. The parents, meanwhile, were having a hard time staying calm and grounded as they tried to figure out what to do. Over time, what we discovered was that many of these families were experiencing chronic sleep deprivation. As we began to ask more pointed questions about families' sleep habits, we learned that a great number of parents were baffled about how to help their children get more sleep, and that many parents were spending an incredible amount of time, day and night, searching for this holy grail. No wonder everyone was in such a lousy mood!

Lack of sleep has long been overlooked as a key contributor to kids' physical and behavioral problems. According to the National Institutes of Health (NIH), "Problem sleepiness has serious consequences. . . . In children, it increases the risk of accidents and injuries. In addition, lack of sleep can have a negative effect on children's performance in school, on the playground, in extracurricular activities, and in social relationships." The NIH further states that "sleep problems are estimated to affect about 70 million Americans of every age, race, and socioeconomic level, and there is a growing body of scientific evidence showing that inadequate sleep results in tiredness, difficulties with focused attention, irritability, easy frustration, and difficulty modulating impulses and emotions. This is as true for children as it is for adults, although little attention has been paid to the problem of sleep in children."

With these staggering statistics, it is critical for parents to get a handle on this issue. Like eating and breathing, sleeping is a fundamental biological function, and a family's well-being depends on all of these basic needs being met. For children *and* parents, trying to get through the day on too little sleep is like trying to get through the day on junk food. At some point your body says, "Hey, I'm in danger here. I don't have enough fuel to keep going." If you don't pay attention and refuel—with sleep or with nutritious food—your body will eventually begin to shut down certain systems, making you feel foggy, groggy, irritable, and tired. If you push too hard and for too long, you'll eventually "crash and burn." This is why we often say that kids and parents who aren't sleeping well aren't getting good "sleep nutrition."

Sleep deprivation takes a toll on each level and layer of a family, including the parents and the child individually, the marriage, and the entire family system. Let's take a closer look at each of these.

Are You Sleep Deprived?

As a famous foursome once sang, "All you need is love." What they forgot to add is, "and a good night's sleep!" After months or years of not sleeping well, both you and your child are likely feeling the effects of chronic sleep deprivation. Do any of these sound familiar?

- You congratulate yourself for being organized enough to be on time for the pediatrician's appointment—only to spend twenty minutes searching the house for your keys.
- You get an overdue notice in the mail from the gas company, though you could swear that you paid that bill last month.
- You find things in your refrigerator that should be classified as science experiments . . . every week.
- You have bumps and bruises all over your body from literally walking into walls in the middle of the night.
- The husband or wife you used to smile sweetly at in the morning upon waking is now either sleeping in another room to actually *get* some sleep, or is a hazy outline of someone with whom you used to talk to about world events, but now resembles the walking dead.

How Sleep Deprivation Affects Your Marriage

Becoming parents is one of the biggest transitions you'll ever go through as a couple, if not *the* biggest. The impact of this monumental event called birth can bring you closer together, or it can cause more stress and conflict than you've ever experienced in your relationship. Your ability to successfully navigate through the initial stages of parenthood and into early childhood and beyond depends on your willingness to look honestly at what you need, as individuals and as a couple, to keep your marriage alive.

While there is a good deal written about the effects of sleep deprivation on babies and children, there is very little written about the effects on *parents* over the long term. As you read this, you may be thinking, "Yeah, yeah, we know it's hard on us, but all we really want to know is how to get our child to sleep. Let's skip to the next chapter." But in working with families over many years, we've seen repeatedly how parents' basic self-care—whether attending to their physical well-being or creating personal downtime—sets the tone in a household for stability and healthy development in the children. There is no area in which this is more important than that of sleep.

In our graduate work, we studied what's called family systems theory. In a nutshell, this theory postulates that when one part of the family system breaks down, the whole system can fall apart. As an example, think of each family member as a spoke in a wheel. If one of those spokes becomes damaged or misaligned, then the whole wheel begins to rotate unevenly. Similarly, if even one family member is off balance, it causes the whole family to be out of balance.

Now let's apply this concept to sleep. When your child isn't sleeping well, you and your spouse, exhausted as well, are likely to feel frustrated, anxious, and irritable with each other. Does this affect your "family wheel" from running smoothly? Most definitely. And when you, as parents, experience those difficult emotions on an ongoing basis, it can't help but affect the way you relate to your child over time. Feeling crummy, though of course you still love your child madly, you might be too tired to feel excited to see her bright and early in the morning, or to have the patience to allow her to happily bang on pots and pans all afternoon. You may even find yourself yelling at your child, due to your short fuse, which then makes her feel guilty and ashamed. Now *you're* feeling guilty, but you can't help it—you're exhausted! When you're overwhelmed and tired, you miss out on many of the joyful moments that come with having a child. Quiet strolls can feel like drudgery, and chasing your toddler around the park can feel far more like work than play.

Here's the good news: *you don't have to live like this!* Let's face it, sleep deprivation can bring out the worst in anyone. Often, parents' sleep is so far off track that they've become depressed or even hostile with each other. Happily, sleep problems often resolve quickly for the families we work with. Children are quite resilient little beings who can easily learn. And as a result, your marriage and your family can thrive.

How Sleep Deprivation Affects You

The issue of self-preservation is equally important as attending to your marriage. When we're working with parents—whether they've just had their first child or their third—we always underscore the importance of each individual parent caring for him- or herself first, even before they turn their attention to the marriage. Why? Well, remember that analogy of the family being like a wheel? You and your spouse are each important spokes of that wheel, and if you aren't taking care of your own needs, then the entire wheel is out of balance. Consider this: on an airplane, when explaining what will happen in case of emergency, flight attendants instruct parents to put on their oxygen masks first and *then* assist their children. Sounds like the opposite of what would come naturally, right? You'd instinctively want to help your child first. But if you *yourself* aren't breathing, you can't help your child. In fact, if you aren't breathing, your child is left alone to fend for herself.

Parents *must* take care of their own needs individually so that they can then care for their marriage, then their children—in that order. If Mom has been feeding, playing with, and helping a child to sleep for days on end without a break, she soon won't have anything left to give. If Dad has been feeling stress and pressure at work with no outlet, he'll feel more irritable and uncooperative at home. Although many parents have a fairly large reserve of love and energy, both Mom and Dad need to rest and refuel with some personal time. Even if you're currently feeling blissfully selfless as a parent, you will eventually crash if you chronically put yourself last on your list.

Finding the Time to Refuel

If you find yourself running on empty, try one of these to help you refuel:

- Ask your spouse to cover for you for a few hours on the weekend, so you can do something for yourself. (By the way, you are *not* allowed to run errands for your child or the household during this time!) Start small if you need to: go to a café and read the newspaper uninterrupted, for example.
- Every so often, take your child somewhere that will tap into your adult side, rather than always choosing a parenting group or the playground. We know it's tough to turn the focus away from him, but he may learn as much by watching you choose fruits and vegetables at the farmer's market as he would at his music class. If you have a toddler or preschooler, take him to a family movie that you can both enjoy, or take a walk together somewhere beautiful (bring a jog stroller for when he gets tired).
- Some gyms have day care. If you like to work out or do yoga, take your child with you and let her have a quick play date while you take an hour to exercise and use the sauna.

- Guess what: it's okay for you to coexist with your baby or child at home once in a while and *not* entertain him. Prop your baby in his infant seat near you with some dangly toys, put some classical music on, and hop into a bubble bath. Get in bed with your preschooler, and tell her it's quiet time. She can bring books to your bed while you read a gossip magazine.
- Help your child learn to be a good sleeper. (That's a gimme!) Once your child sleeps well, you'll have evenings as an optimal time to indulge yourself by watching your favorite TV show, calling your best friend, or even doing a minifacial and plucking your brows. (You may even feel sexy afterward!)

Whatever you choose, pick something that jazzes you, and see how you feel afterward. Then pay attention to how you treat each and every member of your family when you're done. We think you'll be happily surprised.

How Sleep Deprivation Affects Your Child

Parents aren't the only people in the family who suffer from extreme fatigue. If taking care of yourself or your marriage isn't enough motivation to help your child sleep better, then we hope knowing the effects of exhaustion on your little one will be.

Research reported in *Nature Neuroscience* indicates that early brain development, learning, and memory are all supported by good sleep nutrition, while sleep disruption has been linked to behavioral and emotional problems. Most sleep-deprived children show some signs of chronic overtiredness: cranky or fussy behavior, dark circles under the eyes or redness around the eyes, or lots of whining or crying throughout the day. Some children, on the other hand, are miraculously even tempered even when sleep deprived and manage to remain cheerful and happy during the day; be warned, though, that their fatigue is still taking a toll on their development, which can be hard to see.

To develop to their optimum potential physically, emotionally, and cognitively, children need to get the proper amount of sleep for their age; they still do a great deal of developing during sleep in the first few years of life. If they fall short of what they need, kids are deprived of one of the most important foundations they need to be healthy. Usually this deprivation will manifest as decreased alertness, less physical coordination, and increased emotional and behavioral ups and downs throughout the day. Your child's body, brain, and emotions are all affected. And this isn't just a temporary phenomenon. If not resolved, sleep disturbances that start in infancy often continue into later childhood and correlate strongly with emotional, behavioral, and health problems as children grow older. In a long-term study in *The Journal of Child Psychology and Psychiatry*, infants who suffered from chronic sleep deprivation were much more likely at 5 years old and 10 years old to continue suffering from sleep problems than were children who slept well as babies.

A well-rested child, on the other hand—one getting good sleep nutrition—is a thriving child. A rested child will wake up happy to greet the day, maximize her brain power to be able to process all of the stimulation around her and generate creative problem-solving, remain emotionally and behaviorally stable throughout the day, and meet her physical and cognitive needs efficiently, such as mastering the art of balancing on two legs or finding the right words to express herself. But even if you have a child who's a smiling, happy angel in spite of being sleep deprived, you don't want to give her junky sleep nutrition, just as you wouldn't feed her junk food for dinner.

No matter what your child's age, ensuring his good sleep is a vital part of supporting his health. We know you wouldn't intentionally do anything to hinder your child's well-being. We know you want only the best for him and for you, too. That's why you owe it to your entire family to begin getting the sleep you all so desperately need . . . *now*. The rest of this book is dedicated to helping you do just that.

CHAPTER TWO

Creating Your Child's Custom Sleep Plan

Y ou'll want to make sure you read *every word* of this chapter. Reading all of the information contained here is vitally important to our ability to help you as effectively as possible; skimming or skipping even a few paragraphs here or there may mean that you miss an important detail about the best way to help your child sleep—which could cause you to encounter roadblocks or (worst of all) unnecessary crying. If we were sitting with you in your living room, we'd be suggesting you take notes as we talked together, so you could later review the information we'd provided. So as we talk about sleep in this section, whenever you see this symbol ✏ in the text, you'll want to jot down some notes, so you can review them before getting started with sleep learning.

Better yet, you can use the Sleep Planner we've included in Appendix A to track the changes you'll need to make in a very organized manner. Feel free to enlarge and photocopy the Sleep Planner, or download it from the "Tips & Tools" section of our website, www.sleepyplanet.com.

Before You Begin

Before you make your sleep plan and start helping your child learn to sleep, make sure that you and your child are ready to start the process. As your child is learning new sleep skills, you don't want to have any questions about whether she's in pain or discomfort or whether she's struggling with a developmental issue that needs to be tended to first. To ensure smooth sailing from start to finish, here are a few things you'll want to consider.

☑ **Are we all healthy?**

Make sure that your child is completely physically healthy and not cutting a tooth through the gum.

Chronic teething, in which teeth are moving through the gum, is virtually constant throughout infancy and early childhood. During acute teething, however, your child will be in significant discomfort as the tooth prepares to cut through the gum. If your child is about to cut a tooth, you may notice swelling or discoloration on the gum, a low-grade fever, a clear runny nose or diarrhea, or unusually cranky and fussy behavior. This is not a good time to start sleep learning because this teething pain can prevent your child from sleeping well.

Before starting, you'll also want to consult with your pediatrician, who can screen out any pertinent medical issues, including reflux, or discuss the potential side effects of any medications your child may be taking. It's important that you and your spouse are feeling healthy, too, so you'll have the energy to be able to support your child and each other through the sleep-learning process.

☑ **Does my child weigh enough to sleep through the night with a reduction or elimination of feedings?**

Talk to your pediatrician or lactation consultant, especially if you are nursing, about the proper feeding schedule for your child based on age and weight.

If your child has had any sort of weight-gain issues, be sure your doctor is advising you on how to handle nighttime feedings. Most pediatricians advise waiting until 5 months and 15 pounds to wean completely at night. As long as your child is 4 months old and weighs 14 pounds, however, you can safely begin sleep learning as long as you continue offering a dream feed (please see page 38 for more information).

☑ **Has my child just learned an important new skill, or is he going through an important transition?**

Do not start sleep learning if your child has reached a major developmental milestone in the last seven to ten days or is in the middle of adjusting to a significant life change.

Examples of developmental milestones include rolling, crawling, pulling to a stand, walking, or talking up a storm. Reaching a developmental milestone is like winning the lottery for your child; he'll be so revved up with excitement and wanting to practice his new skills that he won't feel much like sleeping—plus, he may also experience some separation anxiety (for more on separation anxiety, see Chapters 7, 8, and 9). Wait to start sleep learning until your child's excitement and anxiety during the day have lessened.

Important transitions for your child include starting preschool, adjusting to a new baby in the home, a move, starting potty training, changing caregivers, and other changes that significantly impact your child's life. Each one of these transitions will profoundly affect your child's emotions, so you don't want to overburden him by asking him to master an important new skill, like learning how to sleep, simultaneously.

☑ Will our schedule allow us to focus on sleep learning for the next week or so?

Make sure that you and your partner will be able to set aside seven to ten days to focus on your child's learning and avoid the distractions of hectic schedules and commitments.

Although your child will likely learn how to sleep well in less than a week, she'll need a little extra time to solidify her new skills. Your ability to commit to helping your child sleep is critical to her ability to learn quickly and cry less. We often say that working on sleep is like going through finals week at college; you may have to put your life on hold temporarily, but when you're finished, you'll be on summer vacation! Many parents choose to start sleep learning on a weekend because their schedules are more flexible and because it's easier to spend time with their child during the day.

☑ How does our regular caregiver feel about helping our child learn how to sleep?

If you have a regular caregiver or day care provider who will be involved in helping your child learn how to sleep, make sure that she will be able to follow the plan exactly as you ask.

If you're helping your child to sleep using one method and your caregiver is doing something different, your child may become confused by mixed messages, which can cause all of your hard work to unravel and your child to cry harder and longer. Write down detailed information, especially for scheduling, bedtime or nap time routines, and how to respond to your child as he learns how to sleep. Plan to make frequent contact with your caregiver during the early days of working on sleep, so you can help troubleshoot any snags that arise.

☑ **Has Mom just returned to work, or is she planning to soon?**

If Mom (or Dad, if he is the primary caregiver) has returned to work in the last two weeks or is within two weeks of doing so, don't start sleep learning.

Your separation from your child is going to be an adjustment all by itself; you'll need the time you do spend together during this transition to be cuddly and easygoing. What's more, a breast-feeding mother often experiences a temporary drop in her milk supply as she adjusts to pumping; working on sleep at the same time could add stress that could further affect milk flow. A good time to start sleep learning is when you have emotionally adjusted to spending less time with your child (and she has, too), when you've fallen into a rhythm with your new schedule and work responsibilities, and when you have no concerns whatsoever about your milk supply.

Customizing Your Sleep Plan

We're now going to help you *customize* a sleep plan for your child, just as we would if we were sitting down with you in our office. No two children are alike, no two families are alike, and therefore no two sleep plans will be exactly alike. We want to help you to identify precisely what isn't working for your particular child so that we know precisely how to help you solve those problems. The more specific your sleep plan is, the easier it will be to follow—and the faster you'll get through the sleep-learning process.

There are seven main "sleep stealers," or reasons your child isn't sleeping well; she may be affected by one of them, by a combination of several, or—if you've hit the jackpot—by all seven.

SLEEP STEALER #1: No Consistent Bedtime Routine

Though most parents know that a bedtime routine is a good idea, it can be hard to be consistent about doing it, either because there's too much to do before bed or because your child has so much energy that it's hard to slow her down. Nonetheless, a predictable wind-down routine is one of the most important tools your child needs to sleep well.

There are several important components of a good bedtime routine:

- **Physical activity should come before the routine.** If Daddy likes to toss the baby in the air, or your toddler likes to streak naked through the living room, go for it! Just make sure you do these activities *before* the bath or bedtime routine, when you'll want to start slowing things down.

- **The routine should last 15 to 60 minutes at nighttime, and about 10 to 15 minutes before a nap.** The length of your routine will depend partly on the age of your child; a 5-month-old might gum a few pages of a board book, whereas an 18-month-old will enjoy at least one full story.

- **Do your bedtime routine in the same room where your child will be sleeping.** It's important that your child spend some time in this space with you, feeling comfortable and relaxed, so the transition into sleep will go smoothly. If you give your child a bath and help him change into pj's in his room, and then return to another part of the house with him for more play or activity, you'll lose the momentum of the wind-down process and will likely find that your child gets a "second wind."

For Working Parents

To help your child transition easily into sleep, try to get home from work early enough to be involved in her entire bedtime routine, so you won't disrupt the process by coming in partway through. If you come home from work later and she's already in her room and feeding quietly, seeing you will excite her and make it much harder to settle into sleep.

- **Do approximately the same activities each night or at nap time, in the same order.** This is what will help your child develop sleep cues, so that over time just doing the routine makes your child sleepy. Wind-down activities can include:
  - A bath
  - A massage
  - Dimming the lights
  - Playing soft music
  - Diaper change and putting on pj's
  - Nursing, a bottle, or a cup of milk
  - A book or song (or several of each)
  - Playing quietly on the floor (no toys that beep or blink)
  - With an older child, talking about your day together

You get the idea. Have fun and be creative; just remember to keep it low-key.

Once you've established a consistent routine, *anyone*—sitter, grandparents, other family—should be able to do exactly what you do to put your child to sleep and have exactly the same results. Mom and Dad are then freed up for a night on the town. Imagine that!

Bedtime Routines for Verbal Children

For your verbal child, be sure to include in your bedtime routine anything she may potentially ask for once you try to leave the room, such as one more sip of water or one more trip to the potty. By ensuring that you take care of these requests before you leave the room, you'll be able to avoid negotiating with her at lights out—and have the peace of mind to know that all her needs have been addressed.

You'll also want to give your verbal child lots of *choices* throughout the routine, such as allowing her to decide which pj's to wear and which books to read. This way, she'll be more likely to cooperate when it's bedtime and she *doesn't* have a choice about that.

Go to the section of your Sleep Planner called "Bedtime Routine Checklist," or grab pen and paper. Decide what you'd like to do in the routine each night and in what order. (Remember, you can download a Sleep Planner on our website at www.sleepyplanet.com under the section entitled "Tips & Tools.")

SLEEP STEALER #2: **Your Child Needs You to Fall Asleep**

It's the most natural thing in the world to rock, feed, or hold your child while he falls asleep. So why doesn't doing this help him *stay* asleep throughout the night? Some children actually can fall asleep on the breast or bottle—or with motion—and then transfer to their crib easily and sleep all night long. Some older children can also fall asleep with Mom or Dad lying next to them in bed without waking in the night. In these cases, there is no sleep problem—and if this describes your situation, by all means continue doing what you're doing, and don't worry about making changes. But many other children who fall asleep with this kind of assistance awaken repeatedly throughout the night, and these disruptions are often caused at least partially by their dependence on certain conditions or activities, or what are called *sleep associations*.

A sleep association is anything your child associates with falling asleep—such as arms holding her; rocking or bouncing; sucking on a pacifier, breast, bottle, or sippy cup; or having a parent lying nearby. Periodically throughout the night, your child drifts up into lighter sleep phases to check out her environment. During these checks,

All Kids Wake Up at Night

Every child has three to five partial awakenings, or arousals, each night. Children who need help getting back to sleep will wake completely during each arousal, crying in distress or appearing at your bedside; those who have learned how to put themselves back to sleep, on the other hand, will never fully wake at all. Falling asleep is a *learned* skill. Some children learn this skill quite easily, while for others it's a bit more difficult.

called "partial arousals," she's not fully conscious—and as long as nothing has changed significantly since she fell asleep in the first place, she simply returns to deeper sleep. But for many children, if something is different, this raises a red flag. Your child's brain signals "crisis," and she cries, calls to you, or comes to your bedside for help. What she needs is for you to re-create the same conditions that were present when she fell asleep in the first place, so she can fall back asleep now. Which you very diligently do!

Imagine your child's perspective. She falls asleep warm and cozy in your arms, sucking on breast or bottle, for instance. Then you tiptoe over to the crib, gently place her inside, and then leave. When she does her first check sometime later, she suddenly realizes, "Oh no! Mommy (or Daddy) was here when I fell asleep, and so was that milk . . . but where's Mommy now? Where's the milk? Help! Someone come in here and do all that stuff again so I can fall back asleep!" It would be like you falling asleep watching TV on the couch, then waking up in your bed, having no idea how you got there. You'd be a bit spooked, too!

Believe it or not, it isn't your child's wake-ups that are the problem. All of us experience partial arousals throughout the night as we assess our sleep environment. If your child is waking all the way up, it's because she doesn't have the ability to put herself *back to sleep,* since she isn't putting herself *to sleep* in the first place. Other children who do put themselves to sleep initially but wake throughout the night have usually developed other associations (for example, someone comes in to feed or to offer comfort) with falling back asleep.

Typical sleep associations include:

• Sucking on a breast, bottle, or pacifier

• Drinking from a sippy cup

- Bouncing, walking, or rocking

- Someone lying down in bed with him

- Music playing

- Watching an aquarium or other stimulating toys with sounds or lights

- Breast-feeding or drinking bottles throughout the night (for a child who's old enough not to feed at night)

Children older than 4 months have the ability to soothe themselves into sleep. There are a variety of things that children may do as they relax, and these skills are hidden inside your child, too, waiting to be discovered. They may include:

- Sucking a thumb or hand

- Gently moving her head from side to side

- Rhythmic kicking or arm movements

- Holding a lovey or stuffed animal

- Finding a favorite comfy position

- Singing or talking

- Sliding his head to the top of the crib for comfort

- Twirling her hair

Not all associations are bad; what's important is that your child can re-create them on his own. So if your child can reinsert the pacifier (each time consistently) or reach for the lovey that was in his hand when he fell asleep, then it's fine for him to continue using them.

What you need to do now is make sure the conditions present when your child falls asleep are the same ones that will be present throughout the night. It doesn't mean you can't feed, rock, or lie next to her at bedtime; it simply means that you can't allow her to *fall asleep* while you do this. "How the heck am I going to do that?" is what you're probably thinking. Scary to imagine, we know. Don't worry, we'll cover all the details in Chapter 3, "Step-by-Step Sleep."

Go to your Sleep Planner and write down what your child's associations are with falling asleep and staying asleep at night. These are the habits we'll help you change, as they're contributing significantly to his wake-ups.

SLEEP STEALER #3: Poor Sleep Environment

Your child's environment plays a very important role in her ability to sleep well. She needs to be protected from disruptions that can prevent her from settling to sleep, sleeping deeply, and sleeping for the right length of time at night and for naps during the day. Keep your Sleep Planner handy as you read, so you can keep track of changes you'd like to make.

What's in the Crib or Bed?

Although your child's *room* should be a place where he feels comfortable and can play, his *crib* or *bed* (and the surrounding area) should be all about sleep. (If you're cosleeping, see page 114.) So whatever is in or around your child's crib or bed that doesn't contribute to sleep—or is a potential safety hazard—should go. This includes:

- **Aquariums, music boxes, or activity boards,** which are distracting and stimulating

- **Bumpers,** as they may cause a suffocation hazard. Breathable, mesh bumpers are fine

- **Large blankets or pillows,** which are dangerous for babies under twelve months and difficult for toddlers or preschoolers to rearrange during the night (if your child sleeps in a bed, though, you'll want to use both)

- **Stuffed animals, books, or toys,** unless your child has a strong attachment to an animal that is safe (has no parts that could be pulled off)

- **Stools or other items** your older child may trip over, if he sleeps in a bed

Light and Dark

On a scale of 1 to 10, 10 being dark, your child's room should be at an 8 or 9 in the morning and during the day for naps. Use blackout shades, or temporarily tack up a heavy blanket or poster board. When your child is learning how to sleep well, you want to give her every environmental chance to do so, and if there's too much light in the room

Check Your Child's Room Temperature

For your child's safety and comfort, the room temperature should range between 68 and 72 degrees. This temperature range will help protect a baby from SIDS risk and prevent your child from waking uncomfortably hot. Although your child's fingers may sometimes feel chilly, as long as the back of her neck is warm, she's fine.

A Word About White Noise

Turn on white noise when your child falls asleep, and make sure it *stays on* throughout the entire sleep period, whether at nighttime or during naps. Once she's a "sleep pro," you can experiment with turning your white noise off.

she may think, "There's a party going on out there somewhere, and I'm not invited. Come get me up, people, so I can be part of the action!"

If your child is old enough to express fear at night, which is common between two and a half and four years, she may feel comforted by a dim overhead light or small nightlight. (See page 189 for a deeper discussion about toddlers, preschoolers, and fears.)

Clothing

Children should be dressed in something warm enough to protect them without a blanket. (Even though children older than 12 months are no longer at risk for sudden infant death syndrome [SIDS], they're so active when they sleep that they kick off blankets during the night.) To ensure your child's warmth, we recommend dressing him in a footed, zip-up "blanket sleeper"; you can layer a onesie or thin pj's underneath if your child's room is especially chilly. For babies over 4 months, we prefer blanket sleepers to sleep sacks, which can frustrate mobile babies whose legs become entangled once they start to roll.

Go to your Sleep Planner and find the "Environmental Checklist." Check off items you'll want to remove from the crib or bed. You'll also want to make a list of things you'll need to arrange (such as room darkening shades over the windows) or purchase (such as a white noise machine) before starting sleep learning.

White Noise

Protect your child from distracting sounds—a ringing phone, beeping horn outside, or barking dog—with some steady white noise. You can use an appliance such as a fan or air purifier, or purchase a white noise machine with volume control (see Resources for where to purchase). Once your child is sleeping better, feel free to see if he can do without it. Some kids, though, will always sleep better with white noise—and although it is technically a sleep association, it's a harmless one as it does not interfere with sleep but actually should enhance it.

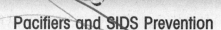

Pacifiers and SIDS Prevention

In 2005, the American Academy of Pediatrics (AAP) suggested that babies under 12 months who use a pacifier while falling asleep may be significantly protected against sudden infant death syndrome (SIDS). However, the AAP also suggested that this benefit was present only when the child used a pacifier upon *falling asleep*, and that parents need not reinsert the pacifier once it falls out. Each family needs to find its own comfort level on using the pacifier while putting their child to sleep; just know that if you do choose to use it, you can allow your child to put himself back to sleep rather than reinserting the pacifier throughout the night.

SLEEP STEALER #4: Misusing Sleep Aids

Sleep aids include pacifiers, swaddling, music and blankies, among other things. Although some sleep aids lead to sleep associations, not all sleep aids are detrimental. What's important is that you know when they are appropriate and when they interfere with sleep.

Not So Fast . . . Going Cold Turkey?

It may be unsettling to think about abandoning the pacifier, swaddle, or music for your child. You may also be feeling overwhelmed by making so many changes all at once. If so, slow it down a bit. Before you begin to implement the changes outlined in the next chapter, you can wean from the swaddle or pacifier and spend a few nights continuing to help your child in other ways. For example, if he is swaddled and used to being rocked back to sleep whenever he wakes, you can start by unswaddling him but continuing to rock him to sleep. Don't worry—we've never yet met a child who couldn't sleep well without these aids.

Pacifiers

If your child uses a pacifier *and* has the ability to reinsert it on his own 100 percent of the time, simply sprinkle six or seven in the crib or place them in a bowl next to his bed so he can always find one. If he's unable to reinsert it on his own consistently, then he'll be dependent on you to help him do so throughout the night. In other words, it's a sleep association, so you'll probably want to stop reinserting it.

Swaddling

It's best to stop using the swaddle after 4 months. Although it's a wonderful tool for helping babies sleep up until this age, it ceases to work well as babies become increasingly mobile. In addition, babies 4 months and older tend to bust out of the swaddle in the middle of the night, which means it also becomes a safety hazard.

Music

Feel free to use music as a part of the wind-down routine, but make sure it's turned off before you put your child down to sleep. After 4 months, music playing throughout the night prevents your child from sleeping as deeply as she needs to.

Transitional Objects or Blankies

Transitional object is a fancy term for a small, breathable blankie (sometimes called a lovey) or child-safe stuffed animal (with no hazardous parts) that serves as a bridge between parent and child when there is separation of any kind. A transitional object can be especially helpful if your child is experiencing any separation anxiety; it gives her a little piece of you to curl up with and feel safe and secure. Even toddlers who have never formed a bond with a favorite toy or lovey can be comforted by a special "Mommy Bear" that the two of you cuddle together at bedtime.

Safety Tip About Blankets

For babies under 12 months old, blankies should be *small* (twelve inches square or smaller) and *breathable* (you can test breathability by putting the bunched up blanket over your face and trying to breathe through it). Even so, there is never a 100 percent guarantee that any object will be safe in your child's crib. If you feel uncomfortable, follow your instincts and don't use a blankie.

The key to using a transitional object correctly is to ensure that the object is small (blankies should be no larger than twelve inches square for babies under 12 months) and fully breathable. If your child hasn't formed an attachment to a blankie or safe stuffed animal, you can encourage her attachment by rubbing it all over your body, saturating it with your scent.

On your Sleep Planner under the section entitled "Review Sleep Aids," check off any changes you'll need to make. If you need to purchase additional pacifiers or would like to try using a transitional object, add these to your list of things to purchase.

If you'd like, sleep with it under your pillow for a few nights. Then, put the object in your child's crib or bed at night and nap time consistently for at least two weeks. Ultimately, it's up to her: she'll either bond with it or she won't. Don't worry if she doesn't; she'll figure out other ways to self-soothe that will work just fine.

SLEEP STEALER #5: Mistimed Sleep Schedule

Although it's sometimes tempting to follow your child's lead and allow him to stay up until he seems tired, there are two reasons that this is one of the surest ways to guarantee a bumpy night of sleep. One reason is that your child will probably wake early, due to morning light; the other is that your child will likely become overtired.

For children of every age, there are optimal "sleep windows" in which it is easiest to drift off into sleep. If your child goes too far past this window—in other words, goes to bed too late for his age—his body becomes stressed and produces a hormone called cortisol. When it comes to helping your child sleep, cortisol is not your friend. It acts as a stimulant, like adrenaline or caffeine; cortisol can cause your child to act "wired" or appear to get a second wind, even when he's overtired. If you've ever wondered how your exhausted child had the energy to run around as though he'd just drunk a pot of coffee, you know what cortisol can do.

Signs Your Child Needs to Go to Sleep

Signs of tiredness can be subtle and easy to miss. They include:

• A glazed look in his eyes
• Resistance to making eye contact
• "Zoning out" behavior
• Lack of interest in activity or interaction with you

Elevated levels of cortisol in your child's system will have three possible effects:

1. He'll have trouble settling into sleep.

2. He'll wake more frequently throughout the night.

3. He'll wake up too early in the morning (meaning so will you).

If only kids could just go to bed later, then magically wake up later in the morning. Ever tried this? It probably backfired because your child was so overtired by the time he finally went to bed that he woke up even earlier than usual.

Signs Your Child Is Overtired

Signs that your child may be *overtired* include:

• Amped-up or wired behavior
• Cranky or fussy mood
• Excessive crying
• Rubbing her eyes
• Red eyes
• Yawning
• Pulling her ears

You know your child best. Start noticing when he seems tired in the evening, and make bedtime 15 to 30 minutes before he begins to show fatigue.

Choosing a Bedtime and Wake Time

Most children do well with a bedtime between 7:00 and 8:00 PM; 8:30 is the *very latest* bedtime we recommend all the way up to age 10.

Choosing a consistent bedtime doesn't mean that your child won't ever be able to stay up late for a special occasion or a family night out; just make sure not to keep him up late for one to two weeks after sleep learning. If he does stay up late one night, try to put him down on time the next.

Most children need at least 11 hours of sleep to function well, so when

A Word about Naps

In Chapter 5, "The Art of the Nap," we'll help you plan your nap schedule based on your child's age. Although we've made a separate chapter for naps, please note that we encourage parents to work on night sleep and nap sleep at the *same time* because it allows the child to practice his new sleep skills more frequently. In other words, you'll begin working on naps the morning after you've completed your first night of sleep learning.

planning your wake time, you should *count forward 11 hours* from when your child goes into his crib or bed. Some children can sleep 10½ hours and seem well rested, while others will sleep 11½ or even 12 hours. How do you determine how much nighttime sleep your child needs? Once he is sleeping through the night, if you find that he wakes after 10½ hours for several days in a row—*and* seems energetic in the morning and stays awake easily till nap time—then you can adjust your schedule accordingly. We've rarely met a child who can sleep only 10 hours and seem well rested. If your child consistently sleeps past 11 hours, lucky you! Just make sure to wake him at the 12-hour mark, so he'll still be able to nap well.

Go to your Sleep Planner and look for the section entitled "My Child's Sleep Schedule." Under bedtime, write down your child's target bedtime. To determine your child's wake time, count forward 11 hours from the bedtime. Example:

Bedtime: 7:30 PM

Wake time: 6:30 AM

Leave naps blank for now (you'll add these in Chapter 5).

Bedtime Means Bedtime

Bedtime is the time when your child is in her crib or bed, the lights go out, and you leave the room. After bedtime, there are no more kisses, cuddles, or chitchat. (You'll have included these in your bedtime routine.)

SLEEP STEALER #6: Limit Testing

(Skip this section if you have a baby younger than 12 months.) Your child may not want to go to sleep. And really, who can blame him? It's so much fun to spend time with Mom and Dad, and he doesn't want to miss the action. What's more, your older child wants more control than he did as a baby; he wants to do things *his* way, whether you want him to or not. Put the two together, and you have a child who will do everything he can to stall, delay, and prolong bedtime.

We often hear stories from parents of toddlers and preschoolers about their children's award-winning performances as they try to delay bedtime. Pulling out all the stops, they act as though they're in the Sahara dying for water, whine that you don't love them if you don't read one more story, or insist that they'll waste away in the middle of the night

Is It Really Limit Testing?

Before you assume that a tantrum is limit-testing behavior, make sure to rule out severe separation anxiety or an important transition in your child's life, such as starting preschool or adjusting to a new baby at home, as the culprit. To learn more, please read the developmental chapter appropriate for your child's age.

unless they have a bedtime snack. If your child isn't highly verbal yet, she may simply tantrum when you try to put her to sleep to see if she can delay your departure. Either way, the drama can be intense and almost always gets a reaction from Mom and Dad. It can be tempting to give in to the demands of your adorable toddler, but delaying bedtime isn't good for her (she needs her sleep) or for you (you need some downtime after a long day and some time with your spouse). With a toddler or young child, it is more important than ever to maintain a loving, predictable bedtime routine, and consistent bedtime boundaries help her feel safe and contained and help her get the sleep she badly needs. As you begin to help your child learn to sleep, be prepared for her creativity; she will likely invent plenty of new reasons why she should not have to go to bed.

Making a Personalized Sleep Book

To help verbal toddlers and preschoolers understand the new limits you're setting around bedtime, you can make a very simple book, illustrated with stick figures, explaining what the changes at bedtime will be. Create this book with your child, asking her to help color in the drawings you make, and use her name frequently so she knows it's about her. Read this book during your routine on the night you begin sleep learning, then every night as your child continues to learn her new skills. In the morning, once you begin working on the changes, you can give your child stickers on a chart for added incentive if you feel that might be helpful.

Here's an example of what a sleep book might include:

"Mommy and Daddy are going to help Emma be a better sleeper, because your body isn't getting enough rest—and if you're not getting good rest, you won't feel like playing during the day."

"After we do your bath and get into PJs, we're going to read books and then sing the Twinkle Twinkle song."

"Then Mommy's going to put you
into your crib (or bed) and say good night,
because it's time for everybody to
get a good night's sleep."

"If you call out after we put you
to bed, Mommy or Daddy will check on you,
but we're not going to (give you a bottle, read
another story)."

"During the night, Emma will sleep in her bed, and Mommy and Daddy will sleep in their bed."

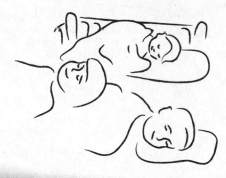

"Your body will feel so much better when you're rested, and then we can have so much fun playing during the day!"

Offering a "Mommy Bear"

Older children sometimes like to have a special "Mommy Bear" or "Daddy Bear" that they can cuddle as they're adjusting to changes in their bedtime routine. This works especially well for children who are used to having a parent stay in the room while they fall asleep. A bear also helps to comfort children while parents gently set new limits around bedtime. You can take your child to the store and allow him to choose an animal himself. Then, at bedtime on the first night you begin sleep learning, you can say, "Mommy won't be able to stay here while you fall asleep this time, but 'Mommy Bear' will be right here to give you hugs all night long."

Offering Choices

It's important to offer verbal children choices in the bedtime routine, so when you do need to set limits when leaving the room, he will feel like he's had some control. Ask your child which pj's he'd like to wear—the red ones or the blue ones? Allow him to pick out which story he'd like, and be sure to ask whether he'd like one more sip of water or whether he needs to use the potty (if appropriate). You can end with something like, "How many kisses would you like before bed—three or four?" (not twenty-five!). These final choices about water and potty should be offered immediately before the actual bedtime. Then, when it's bedtime, there are no more choices and no more discussions.

Using a Safety Gate

Children who sleep in beds but have difficulty staying in their rooms at bedtime may benefit from having a safety gate installed at the door. Gates create a boundary much like a crib railing but don't confine your child and frighten her the way a closed door might. (We do not advocate holding a door closed as a child attempts to get out, as this can traumatize her and make her feel fearful about being in her room and bed.) In essence, having a gate at your child's door is like creating a big crib out of her room. She can still look out over the top of the gate or through it (to see light in the hallway, for instance), but she'll be contained safely in her room. (Don't worry; you'll be checking on her regularly as she learns how to sleep. We'll explain how in the next chapter, "Step-by-Step Sleep.") If you decide to use a gate, let your child help you with the installation of the gate and tell her that it's not safe for little children to walk around the house at night, so the gate will help her stay safe in her room.

Preempting Requests After Lights Out

You'll want to include in your bedtime routine anything your child may potentially ask for once you try to leave the room, such as water or one more trip to the potty. Tell her that you're placing a sippy cup by her crib, and invite her to use the potty one last time after your story. This way, you'll be able to avoid negotiating with your child after lights out—and you'll have the peace of mind to know that all her needs have been addressed.

Get a gate that has vertical slats and doesn't have places where little feet can dig in to climb. Also, find a gate that attaches to the doorway or wall with hardware versus one that uses pressure, which can be pushed over by a determined child. Secure the gate high enough in the door that your child cannot climb over it, and remove any stools, chairs, or other objects from your child's room that she could use to hoist herself over the top of the gate.

Alternative to Using a Safety Gate

If you'd rather not use a safety gate to help your child stay in her room during sleep learning, you can simply walk her back to bed each time she gets up. Be aware, however, that a child may need to be returned to her room constantly on the first several nights before she understands the new rules at bedtime. Often, children who have the freedom to leave their rooms will use every trick in the book to get you to go back to helping them to sleep. We'll explain in detail how to help your child sleep without using a gate in Chapter 3, "Step-by-Step Sleep."

On your Sleep Planner, write down your child's typical limit-testing behaviors. These may include tantrums (for less verbal children) or asking for more water or for you to lie down with her. Seeing these on paper can help you stay focused when you begin the sleep-learning process, so you'll remember that she's not in urgent need of assistance. In addition, write down the things you'll need to prepare to help your child minimize his discomfort with new limits (such as making a special sleep book, using a "Mommy Bear," or installing a safety gate).

SLEEP STEALER #7: Night Noshing

(Skip this section if you have a child who is no longer feeding at night, and go to "Review Your Sleep Plan" on page 51.) To be successful in learning how to sleep—and to learn as quickly as he can—your child needs to have one clear, consistent response to his night wakings. If you sometimes feed him when he cries and some-times do not, he'll become confused and will cry longer and harder overall. Our method of weaning is designed to greatly mini-mize, and often eliminate, any crying around weaning feedings. Please note that if your baby is under 5 months or weighs less than 15 pounds, you'll want to continue to offer one "dream feed" before you go to bed: gently rouse the baby just enough to feed (it's okay if he's not fully awake in these cases), then put him right back down again when he's done. Because you've roused him out of sleep, he may fuss briefly but should return to sleep again quickly.

Babies Younger Than 12 Months

You may be wondering how your baby will make it all the way through the night without feeding. You have every reason to be concerned about this if your child is used to eating at night. But by the time a baby is 5 months old and weighs 15 pounds, she should be able to sleep till morning wake time without a feed. (Remember to check with your doctor to make sure you're on the same page about your child's feedings at night.)

Formula-fed babies may be ready to wean nighttime feeds ear-lier than breast-fed babies, as formula tends to stay in a baby's sys-tem longer. If you're breast-feeding, check with your doctor and/or lactation consultant before weaning at night to make sure your milk supply is adequate during the day so your body will adjust properly to the increased demand for daytime feedings. Also, make sure that your baby is gaining weight appropriately, as some babies may still need at least one feeding at night till they're a bit older.

At 5 months and 15 pounds, if your baby is still feeding at night, she is legitimately hungry out of habit—in other words, she's used to eating something—and is taking part of her 24-hour milk requirement at night rather than during the day. The good news: it is now possible for you to *transfer* your nighttime feeds to daytime feeds (not eliminate them) through a slow weaning process.

Toddlers 12 Months and Older

If you have a toddler over 12 months old who is growing well, he is perfectly capable of taking in all of the calories and hydration that he needs during the day. (Exceptions: when your child is sick, if he has allergies that cause him to cough, or if he is taking medication that can increase thirst, he may need additional hydration at night.) Dentists cringe when they hear that older children are still feeding during the night, as the milk pools on developing teeth and can cause decay. What's more, large quantities of milk or water at night can cause children to have soggy, leaky diapers in the morning (or before).

If your older child is still waking at night for either milk or water, tell him that you have made a decision to stop giving him milk at night and that you'll check on him if he wakes up, but that he should hug his lovey or bear and go back to sleep. We sometimes recommend that our parents tell their child that the "Sleep Teacher" said that it's not good for him to drink milk at night anymore. Information coming from a teacher may sound more official.

"But She's Thirsty!"

If you absolutely can't fathom the idea that your toddler can make it through the night without a sip of water, put a sippy cup or bottle of water in her crib, and tell her that if she gets thirsty, she can take a sip and go back to sleep.

Making Your Weaning Schedule If You Are Breast-Feeding

Look back over the last week or so. Take note of when your child tended to feed at night, and for approximately how many minutes. If the timing of the feeds tends to vary, use the *earliest* time for each feed. If you're not sure about the length of time, approximations are okay, but try to *overestimate* when in doubt, so your child won't be unnecessarily hungry; if he sometimes feeds for 10 minutes but sometimes it's closer to 5, for example, consider what the length has been *more than half of the time*. If your child wakes often throughout the night but sometimes doesn't feed for more than 2 minutes before returning to sleep, your child is pacifying rather than eating, so this doesn't count as a feed.

Here's a typical night for 8-month-old Matthew, who weighs 18 pounds:

8:00 PM	Bedtime
11:30 PM	Breast-feed 10 minutes
1:00 AM	Breast-feed 2 minutes
2:00 AM	Breast-feed 2 minutes (plus rocking)
3:30 AM	Breast-feed 8 minutes
7:00 AM	Wake time

In this case, Matthew woke four times each night during the past week. Let's say that sometimes Matthew ate for only 7 or 8 minutes at the 11:30 feed, but more than half the time, he ate for closer to 10 minutes. To be conservative, his parents should set 10 minutes as a starting point for weaning. Although Matthew ate briefly at 1:00 and 2:00, we would not need to wean these feeds as they are 2 minutes long and thus have more to do with pacifying than with eating. This baby's significant feedings—the ones his parents would need to wean—are at 11:30 (10 minutes) and 3:30 (8 minutes).

Once you start to work on your child's sleep, you'll plan to wake and feed her about an *hour* before she usually wakes; then, starting with the maximum amount of time you've been feeding, you'll subtract 2 minutes per feeding each night, thus gradually reducing her intake. (If you prefer to be more conservative, you can subtract only 1 minute each night.) Using Matthew's information as an example, his parents would do the following on the first night:

- Wake Matthew at 10:30 PM (1 hour before he normally wakes at 11:30 PM) and feed him for 8 minutes (2 minutes less than 10, the usual length of time).

- Set the alarm for 2:30 AM (1 hour before Matthew typically wakes at 3:30 AM) and feed for 6 minutes (2 minutes less than 8, the usual length of time).

On the second night, Matthew's parents would do the following:

- Wake Matthew at 10:30 PM and feed for 6 minutes, then wake him again at 2:30 AM and feed him for 4 minutes.

On each subsequent night, Matthew's parents would continue to drop each feeding by 2 minutes. After reducing a feed down to 2 minutes, Matthew would be finished with that feed, and it would be eliminated the next night.

Pacing Nighttime Feeds

If the length of your child's feeding is widely variable at night, start with the *longest* amount of time your child has fed in the last week and subtract 1 or 2 minutes per feeding each night. If your child's feed times are unpredictable, pinpoint the *earliest* time your child has woken in the last week and plan to wake and feed her 1 hour earlier than that time. You can then space the rest of her nighttime feeds equally throughout the night; for example, if your child typically feeds three times a night, you can plan to wake her at 9:30 PM, 12:30 AM, and 3:30 AM.

Now let's incorporate your weaning schedule into your overall sleep plan based on the above example. Here's how Matthew's complete nighttime schedule might now look:

8:00 PM Bedtime
10:30 PM Feed for 8 minutes
2:30 AM Feed for 6 minutes
7:00 AM Wake time

Night 2

8:00 PM Bedtime
10:30 PM Feed for 6 minutes
2:30 AM Feed for 4 minutes
7:00 AM Wake time

Night 3

8:00 PM	Bedtime
10:30 PM	Feed for 4 minutes
2:30 AM	Feed for 2 minutes
7:00 AM	Wake time

Night 4

8:00 PM	Bedtime
10:30 PM	Feed for 2 minutes
	(no 2:30 AM feed—Matthew has
	finished weaning this feeding)
7:00 AM	Wake time

Night 5

8:00 PM	Bedtime
	(no feeds—Matthew has
	successfully weaned at night!)
7:00 AM	Wake time

As they are slowly, methodically weaned at night, most breast-fed babies will naturally transition their hunger to the daytime and either want to nurse more frequently or nurse for a bit longer at each feed. However, it's very important to make an effort to feed a baby younger than 12 months more often as you are weaning at night to ensure that he is taking in the proper amount of milk and to ensure that your milk supply remains adequate. If your child is eating solids, he may also choose to eat more during each meal (though if your baby is under 12 months, remember that milk is the primary nutrition source; don't let your child eat so much solid food that he refuses to take the proper amount of milk for his age and weight).

Making Your Weaning Schedule If You Are Bottle-Feeding

Take a look back over the last week or so. Note when

A Word About Caffeine and Nursing

Breast-feeding moms, watch your caffeine intake as you are helping your baby learn how to sleep. Eliminating caffeine from your diet is the best option, but if you must consume caffeine, try to do so early in the day, or consider using stored breast milk for the feed following your caffeine intake and "pumping and dumping" for that particular feed.

your child tends to feed at night, and how many ounces she eats each time. If the timing of the feeds tends to vary, use the *earliest* time for each feed. If you're not sure about the amount of intake for each bottle, approximations are okay, but try to *overestimate* when in doubt, so your child won't be unnecessarily hungry; if she sometimes eats 4 ounces and sometimes it's closer to 6, for example, use 6 ounces as a starting point. If your child wakes often throughout the night but sometimes doesn't eat more than 2 ounces before returning to sleep, your child is pacifying rather than eating, so this doesn't count as a feed.

In the following example, Emma, who is 5 months and 15 pounds, wakes three times at night to feed.

7:00 PM Bedtime

10:30 PM Feed 5 ounces

12:20 AM Feed 1 to 2 ounces

3:30 AM Feed 4 ounces

6:00 AM Wake time

In this case, Emma has two significant feeds and one feed at 12:20 AM that simply serves to pacify her back to sleep (because it's 2 ounces or less). So the important feeds to wean are the 10:30 PM and 3:30 AM feedings. On the first night, Emma's mom would wake her 1 hour earlier than when she'd normally wake—at 9:30 PM and 2:30 AM—and offer one ounce less each night per feed. After Emma has drunk only one ounce on a particular night, she has successfully weaned that feed, and it is eliminated the following night.

Here's what Emma's new schedule would look like:

Night 1

7:00 PM Bedtime

9:30 PM Feed 4 ounces

2:30 AM Feed 3 ounces

6:00 AM Wake time

Night 2

7:00 PM Bedtime
9:30 PM Feed 3 ounces
2:30 AM Feed 2 ounces
6:00 AM Wake time

Night 3

7:00 PM Bedtime
9:30 PM Feed 2 ounces
2:30 AM Feed 1 ounce
6:00 AM Wake time

Night 4

7:00 PM Bedtime
9:30 PM Feed 1 ounce
6:00 AM Wake time

Night 5

7:00 PM Bedtime
6:00 AM Wake time

As your bottle-fed child reduces nighttime ounces, offer an ounce or 2 ounces more per bottle during the day if she's under 12 months, or more solids if she's over 12 months.

This way, she'll continue taking in the same amount of food in a 24-hour period, but she'll be drinking or eating during the day instead of at night.

In the section of your Sleep Planner called "My Child's Weaning Schedule," write down the time of the feeding(s) and the number of minutes or ounces you will feed one your child on Night 1. If you're weaning more than one feeding, fill in the chart for your subsequent feeds. Then fill in the decreasing number of minutes or ounces for Night 2, and so on.

Commonly Asked Questions About the Weaning Process

Here are some of the most frequent questions parents ask about this process.

Q: How do I know how many ounces my bottle-fed baby needs a day?

A: A handy way to figure out how much your bottle-fed baby needs to eat is to divide his weight by three; your baby should drink this many ounces at minimum, four or five times a day, to continue gaining weight appropriately. (Note: if your baby is both breast- and bottle-fed, you cannot use this method, as breast-feeds cannot be quantified.)

For example: Erica weighs 15 pounds and is strictly bottle-fed. If we divide her weight by three, we get 5 ounces, four or five times a day, for a total of

20 to 25 ounces. So to continue gaining weight appropriately, Erica needs to eat a minimum of 20 to 25 ounces in a 24-hour period. If your baby is eating solids and taking in less milk than her minimal requirement, talk to your doctor. You may want to reduce the solids so that she'll be hungry enough to drink the minimum amount of appropriate milk. Most pediatricians believe that until 12 months, breast milk or formula remains the primary source of nutrition, and solids should take a backseat.

Q: Wouldn't it be easier to just stop feeding cold turkey, without weaning?

Be Careful of Mixed Messages in the Morning

Sometimes, as parents begin to enjoy success with night sleep, their child will initially continue to wake at 4:00 or 5:00 AM. We're often asked whether it's okay to feed him at this time, so he'll go back to sleep for a bit. Be careful! If you answer your child's wake-up with a feed at any time before your scheduled wake time, he is *still* getting a mixed message—and what often happens is that the 4:30 AM wake-up creeps earlier and earlier, to 4:00, 3:30 . . . you get the idea. If you've established that your child is old enough and weighs enough not to eat at night, he'll do just fine with daytime feeds only, or with daytime feeds and one "dream feed" before you go to bed.

A: On the face of it, it might seem easier just to drop your feeds altogether. When a child is accustomed to drinking milk at night, however, she needs to transition that intake to the daytime, but she needs to do so slowly to ensure that she won't wake hungry *out of habit* in the middle of the night. Using our weaning methods, you'll never wonder whether your child is crying out of hunger. Dropping feeds suddenly can also cause engorgement and discomfort for breast-feeding moms.

Q: My child is finally sleeping—how can I possibly wake him?

A: We've all heard that adage "Never wake a sleeping baby." So why would you—especially now that he's finally sleeping? It's okay to do so in this case because we're recognizing that even though a child who is at least 5 months and 15 pounds doesn't *need* to eat at night, he's used to doing so and thus is hungry out of habit. By waking him first and beating him to the punch, you will prevent him from rousing himself out of a deep sleep to eat and will avoid reinforcing his wake-up with a feed on demand. Almost always, the child settles again immediately after being woken for a feed. If for any reason he does not, remind yourself that you have weaned him *slowly*, and his fussing is not due to hunger. Respond to him by using our methods for checking in outlined in the next chapter (or one of the alternative methods in Chapter 6).

Q: What if my baby is the right age and weight for night weaning, but I'd like to give him one nighttime feed . . . just in case?

A: If you feel like you're just not ready to wean yet, but you'd still like to improve your child's sleep, you can choose to keep a "dream feed" going indefinitely—in other words, you can wake your child sometime before you go to bed and top her off for the night with a breast- or bottle-feed. What is most important is that *you* wake your child to feed and avoid feeding her when *she* wakes, so she doesn't get confused by mixed messages—that sometimes you come to feed her when she cries, and sometimes she needs to get herself back to sleep. Responding to your child inconsistently will make the crying—and the whole process of getting great sleep—go on much longer than necessary.

Q: **What if my baby seems too sleepy to feed and will not take enough milk?**

A: Try to rouse him gently enough that he starts to suck. If he does not take the full amount at the scheduled feeding time, wait another hour and try again.

Review Your Sleep Plan

Now that you've created your plan, review it with everyone who will be involved in making changes with your child's sleep so that you all clearly understand what the plan is. Choose your start date and prepare as necessary. Chapter 3 will guide you step by step through implementing your plan. You're getting closer to great sleep!

CHAPTER THREE

Step-by-Step Sleep

A few hours before you begin working on your child's sleep, make sure that your Sleep Planner or notes are handy and legible for quick reference when you're groggy in the middle of the night. Review your plan thoroughly, especially if it's been more than a day or two since you created it. Make sure that all of the things you'll need to ensure your child's good sleep are in place; this includes having already darkened the room, arranged for white noise, created a book with your child, or prepared a safety gate at the door for a child who sleeps in a bed. Being well organized will ensure that you get through the sleep-learning process as quickly as possible and with a minimum of crying.

You'll want to read this entire chapter through before starting, so you'll know what to do at each moment along the way. Then, as you're helping your child sleep over the course of a few nights and days, refer back to the steps we've outlined as often as you need to.

Take a deep breath. You're probably feeling some anxiety as you think about making changes. Just remember that thousands of children have successfully learned how to sleep using these methods—and yours will, too.

Begin Your Sleep Plan at *Night*

If your child still naps, begin sleep learning at night rather than trying to first tackle naps, which can take longer to straighten out. You also don't want to have a whole day of bumpy naps (and they usually are bumpy the first day) and then try to put your child to bed that night overtired; if he is overtired, he'll cry more and take longer to fall asleep. (Remember, we encourage parents to work on night sleep and nap sleep simultaneously, meaning you begin with night sleep first and then start working on naps the next day. We'll help you tackle naps in Chapter 5, "The Art of the Nap.")

Step 1:

Create Your Station

Somewhere near your child's room—perhaps in the living room or your bedroom—set up your sleep station with the following items:

✓ A digital clock

✓ A pen

✓ Your Sleep Planner or notes

✓ The Sleep Chart (see Appendix C) to record your child's activity and progress (you can also go to our website, www.sleepyplanet.com, and download the Sleep Chart from our "Tips & Tools" section)

✓ This book, with both this section and Appendix B: "Crying 911"
bookmarked

✓ Your baby monitor, if you use one

✓ Tissues (and have a big carton of the richest, most sinful ice cream you can find ready in the freezer!)

This sleep station is *essential* for helping you follow your plan correctly. If you forget what you're supposed to be doing in the middle of the night and inadvertently give your child inconsistent or mixed messages, he will sleep less and cry more. Also, writing down all the details throughout your child's learning process will help you see progress on a daily basis. Noting his improvement from one day to the next will help you to stay motivated to achieve your goals.

Preparing Your Verbal Child for Sleep Changes

A few hours before you begin your bedtime routine on the first night of making changes, walk your child through a mock routine and bedtime. Show her where you'll be sleeping (in your bedroom), and if she's sleeping in a bed, remind her what will happen if she gets up (you'll walk her back to her room or check on her at the gate; see Step 4 for guidelines). If you are using a safety gate, tell your child that if she stays in bed, you'll leave the gate open (as long as the rest of your house is safety proofed), but if she gets out of bed, you'll need to close the gate to make sure she's safe in her room. This way, *her* behavior determines whether the gate stays open or closed—and because she has the choice, she'll feel more empowered and thus more likely to cooperate.

Step 2:

Do Your Bedtime Routine

The *most* important thing to remember about your routine is to *make sure your child does not fall asleep* under the same old conditions he's used to (such as while rocking or feeding or while you stay in the room). So if your child is used to falling asleep on the breast or bottle, on the first night you start, pull him off the minute you begin seeing the "drunken sailor" signs: heavy eyelids, slowed-down movement, losing consciousness fast. When this happens, give him a little bit of motion: "Honey-honey-honey! We can't fall asleep just yet." Crack the window, and get some fresh air in there. Keep the lights a little higher the first couple of nights. Tickle his feet, talk to him in a silly voice—do anything you need to do to make sure he *does not fall asleep* before you put him down. It's not enough to wake your child after he's dozed for a few minutes; once he's taken even a little dip into dreamland, his brain and body begin operating in "shutdown" mode, and he'll be mighty angry upon being woken again—and have a much harder time resettling (in other words, he'll cry more).

At some point during your routine, have a little chat with your child. Say, "Okay, honey, we're going to do things a little differently tonight because it's time for us to help you learn to be a really good sleeper. We're going to put you in your crib (or bed) awake, and then you're going to learn

Reading Your Sleep Book with Your Verbal Child

If you have a verbal child, as part of your routine you'll want to read the special sleep book you made together (for more on making this book, see page 32 in Chapter 2). If your child begins to protest while you read about the changes, calmly say, "I know you like (the milk, for mommy to stay in the room while you fall asleep), but it's time to stop. I know that feels hard." Empathy can go a long way in helping a child to feel better understood. Remind him that he'll be able to hold his lovey or hug his "Mommy Bear" if he misses you during the night.

how to put yourself all the way to sleep. We know it'll be a little hard at first, but you can do it. Mommy and Daddy will be right here to help you." She may not understand most of what you're saying if she's pre-verbal, but she can sense your calm and loving tone of voice. We believe it's respectful to communicate to a child when making changes, and staying calm as you're talking about them (even if you're feeling a little jittery yourself) helps your child to calm herself as well.

Step 3:

Put Your Child in the Crib or Bed Awake

After you've done the last bit of your bedtime routine with your child still awake, put her into her crib or bed. Say, "Okay, sweetie, it's time to go to sleep. We know you can do it, and we love you!" Leave the room.

No More Choices!

If you have a verbal child who begins to protest, tell him lovingly that he's had lots of choices already and that choice time is all done.

Breathe. We know, your heart is breaking. Okay, let's be honest: it feels like somebody ripped your heart out of your chest and is doing the cha-cha on top of it. But remember, it is *absolutely critical* that your child go to bed awake so she can learn how to be a great self-soother and so she can understand that you have set new rules around bedtime.

Yikes . . . My Child Is Crying!

You've just put your child down awake, and she is crying in frustration or protest. Every bone in your body is telling you to just get her, hold her, and soothe her. Of course you feel this way! You are a caring, loving parent, and we'd honestly be worried if you weren't feeling at least a couple of tugs on your heartstrings. (And it probably feels more like your heart is being yanked from your chest.)

On a daily basis for over a decade, we've helped countless parents through this very difficult moment. You may be thinking, *What if she's emotionally damaged after crying? What if she never trusts me again?* Your natural inclination is to just soothe her. And yet, you've been doing that—for weeks, months, or years—and that hasn't helped her sleep. What's more, the long-term effects of sleep deprivation are far worse than a few days of your child's frustration in learning a new skill or accepting a new limit.

After much experimentation with lots of different methods, we've found that the ones we offer you here do the *best* job of minimizing your child's overall crying and frustration—if you can stay very consistent. Right now, promise yourself you only need to hang in there for one night. Like the parents we've worked with, though, we think you'll find that in the morning, your child is as happy to see you as always.

Remember, most children who learn how to sleep using our methods are sleeping well in less than five nights—and there are usually far fewer tears each night. This is *short-term* solution to fix a long-term problem. You are a loving, attentive parent who wants what's best for your child, and right now the most loving thing you can do for him is to stand back, for a few minutes at a time, and allow him to learn the critical skill of falling asleep, or for older children, learn to accept changes or new limits around bedtime. Hug him and kiss him non-stop tomorrow, and for tonight, try to stay the course.

We'll address crying in more detail in Chapter 4, "The Truth about Crying," and you'll also find answers to frequently asked questions about crying in Appendix B, "Crying 911: Emergency Help for Panicked Parents."

Check In on Your Child

It's important to give your child *a few minutes*, unassisted, to begin to learn how to soothe herself to sleep. She needs this time to begin learning her new skills, and giving her some space will help her learn fastest with the fewest tears. The most effective intervals to wait before checking in on your child, we've found, are 5 minutes to start, then 10, and then every 15 minutes until she falls asleep; this is a good balance between giving her an opportunity to learn new skills while reminding her with love that you're still there to support her. If 5 minutes feels too long to wait, though, feel free to start smaller, such as with 3 minutes. Please know, however, that although it feels good to see her more often, frequent check-ins may have the unfortunate effect of causing your child to cry longer and harder, because she sees you coming in and out of the room more often. Nonetheless, choose intervals that feel right for you—and then stick with them. In other words, don't wait 10 minutes, then go back to 5 or 3.

For Crib Sleepers

- Go to your sleep station and use your Sleep Chart to write down the date and time that you've put your child to bed. What's happening? Your child is probably crying. (Ouch . . . this is the hard part!)

> ### Key Points to Reduce Protest Crying During Check-Ins
>
> 1. Wait the **exact** interval you've set for your check-ins.
> 2. **Don't touch** your child, which will tease her into thinking you'll help her to sleep.
> 3. **Use a calm, loving tone of voice** as you support her.
> 4. Stay just **30 seconds** maximum.

- Wait 5 minutes (or your designated first check-in interval) before checking on your child. This will probably feel like an eternity! While you are waiting, do whatever you need to do to take care of yourself—eat some ice cream, squeeze your spouse's hand (try not to cut off the circulation), call friends who have helped their children learn how to sleep successfully. If you can, try to send your child love and calming thoughts—even though she can't hear or see you right this second, you can still communicate with her, whether out loud or in your heart. Here's a great idea: while you're waiting, read Appendix B: "Crying 911" for support.

- When it is time for the first check-in, go halfway into your child's room—close enough that he can see and hear you but not close enough to touch—and say, "Honey, Mommy (or Daddy) is here, and it's okay to go to sleep. I love you so much, and I'll check on you again in a little while." *Don't linger longer than 30 seconds*, as doing so will tease him into thinking you will pick him up and will make him cry harder. Don't worry, you'll check in again soon to remind him that you haven't disappeared and that you are right there to support him. As you talk, your voice should sound positive and loving, not tense or doubtful, so you may need to give your best Oscar-caliber performance to sound reassuring. (If you need to have a good cry, go right ahead—but wait till you've left the room.)

- Leave the room and record your check-in at the sleep station. Then wait the next designated interval and check in again, supporting your child with your loving voice and presence. The third interval is the longest you'll have to wait; continue to check in at this interval until your child falls asleep. Each time you check in, write it down.

No Cheating!

Do not cheat and check in prior to the next designated interval. Each minute that you wait counts tremendously toward your child's ability to go to sleep—and checking in too often will likely cause him to cry longer and harder than he otherwise would have.

For Bed Sleepers Using a Safety Gate

Your child will likely pop out of bed immediately after being put down. When she does, walk her back to bed and explain calmly—without sounding angry!—that you'll need to close the gate to help keep her safe in her room. Leave quickly to avoid getting pulled into negotiation with your child. Then proceed to do the check-ins as explained above, but instead of going into the room, go close enough to the gate that your child can see and hear you but not close enough to touch. Do your check-ins from this position.

Extending Your Check-Ins

If your child seems to cry much harder when you check in, you may want to extend your next check-in interval by an *additional* 5 minutes (or longer if you'd like). Toddlers especially can sometimes benefit from longer intervals, as seeing you more often may aggravate them and make them angrier than they would have been if they just had a few more uninterrupted minutes to fall asleep.

Watch for Clues That Your Child Is Learning

If your child is whining or complaining and not crying—or if his cries are intermittent, with pauses of more than 30 seconds—try not to check on him, even if it's time. These are indications that he is learning, and seeing you at this critical moment in his progress will likely only escalate his crying. If he does begin crying hard again, start your checks again, repeating the last interval you used.

For Bed Sleepers Not Using a Safety Gate

When your child gets out of bed, say matter-of-factly, "Oops, you got out of bed—let Mom (or Dad) walk you back." Put him back down, then leave the room again without further discussion. This can feel tough to do because your child may tantrum. He is not used to these new boundaries and wants to go

Try the Tag-Team Approach

Either Mom or Dad can do the check-ins or walk your child back to bed; just don't both participate at the same time, which is too stimulating. You can take turns, or just one of you can support your child if doing so is harder on the other parent.

back to "the old way." Continue to walk your child back to bed each and every time he comes out of his room—which can be quite a few times the first night—and try to eliminate any talking after the first couple of times, so your child won't have any incentive to continue getting up. This method requires absolute calm on your part, as any reaction from you—even mild frustration—will only reinforce and continue the behavior. Be prepared: he will do everything he can to get you to cave in and help him, just as you always have! If you can hang in there and stay consistent, though, your child will eventually put himself to sleep.

Key Points to Reduce Protesting While Walking Your Child Back to Bed

1. **Don't allow yourself to get pulled into conversation** with your child, which will give her incentive to stay awake and cause her to protest for longer.

2. **Avoid caving in to demands for water,** a hug, and the like. You'll have already offered these at bedtime.

3. **Don't express your anger or frustration to your child,** which will reinforce his protesting. If you need to take a break, allow the other parent to take over.

4. **Leave the room quickly** each time you return your child to bed.

Why Can't I Hold My Crying Child?

You're probably thinking that it's hard enough to imagine listening to your child cry, but the thought of not holding her as she does so seems unbearable. On the surface, not holding your crying child doesn't feel right—and that's why we always say that helping a child sleep is one area of parenting where you may not be able to follow your instincts and have it all work out fine. Your instincts to care for her are correct—but remember, you've been picking her back up, rocking her, or lying down with her, and none of that has helped her sleep well. Now, in helping her learn to sleep more independently, your caring for her means giving her a little bit of uninterrupted time and space to begin learning one of the most important skills she needs to thrive: learning how to fall asleep unassisted.

Tame the Tension

While you are waiting as your child learns, try not to stand outside her door, tense and nervous. Stay nearby, but do something to relax: take some

How Long Will This Take?

The average amount of time a child protests the first night before falling asleep is about an hour (as you continue to support him with check-ins or by walking him back to bed), but it's also normal for a child to persist a bit more. Some take longer than others, while some surprise their parents and learn more quickly. The first night is almost always the hardest, because your child is adjusting to changes. But your child will generally cry less each night, and each night that you can stay consistent means that you'll have taken a giant leap toward getting great sleep *every* night.

deep breaths, clean out your purse, get a hug from your spouse. Another idea is to send your child calming, loving thoughts, envisioning her sleeping peacefully.

Step 5:

Sleep at Last!

Once your child falls asleep (hooray!), record the total amount of time it took her to do so. For those of you with babies, you've made a significant amount of progress already, because your child has already begun to learn her new skill; now she just needs to perfect it. For toddlers or preschoolers who are used to protesting at bedtime, not only have they now learned to fall asleep unassisted, but—with your calm consistency—they have also taken a giant step forward in being able to accept new rules around bedtime.

Move your sleep station with you wherever you'll be for the rest of the evening. If you decide to go to bed (not the worst idea), bring the sleep station and your Sleep Planner with you so you can continue to record information during the night.

Remember, this is a *temporary* process to fix a difficult problem. Allowing your child to cry or feel frustrated is not your new parenting style, and you won't have to allow it for long if you stay consistent. Once your child is sleeping well in a few nights, you'll be thankful you hung in there. (And tomorrow, you can kiss her all day long!)

"But What If She's Hungry?"

If you are worried that your child is hungry at an early hour, pick an earlier time to wake and feed her, then wean that feed (see Chapter 2, "Sleep Stealer #7: Night Noshing").

Night Weaning

If you're weaning your baby or toddler at night, be sure to check your Sleep Planner before you go to bed to remember when you are scheduled to wake and feed your child; you might also want to review the section in Chapter 2 entitled "Sleep Stealer #7: Night Noshing." Set your alarm on *high volume* to make sure you'll wake up. At each of your designated feed times, simply go in and gently get your child up. You do not need to wake him fully! He needs to be only awake enough to be able to take in the right amount of milk. This is different from putting your child down to sleep in the first place, because *you're* rousing him out of sleep this time, only enough to feed. Burp him if you need to after the feed, then put him back down. Almost always, kids go right back down without a peep. If he does fuss, it probably won't last more than a minute or two; if necessary, however, you can begin doing your check-ins.

"What If He Wakes Up Before It's Time to Feed Him?"

If your child happens to wake just before a scheduled feed (for instance, he wakes at 1:45 AM, and you're scheduled to feed at 2:00), *do not* feed your child at this time. Instead, do your check-ins, let him put himself back to sleep, then wait 10 or 15 minutes, wake him, and feed. You want to respond to him *every time he wakes* with one clear, consistent message; if sometimes he cries and you do check-ins, and sometimes he cries and you feed, he'll become confused and then cry harder and longer whenever he wakes, hoping you'll feed him. Remember, you're feeding your child approximately an hour earlier than he's used to eating—so although he may be ready for a snack earlier than you expected, he won't starve.

How to Handle Night Wakings

You're in bed, asleep. For once, everyone in the house is asleep—or so you thought. Yes, that's your little one, waking up out of habit! Whether this is 9:00 PM or 2:00 AM—anytime between your designated bedtime and wake time, *not* one of your feeding times (see the previous section for more on those)—here's what to do.

For Crib Sleepers

- At your sleep station, write down what time your child woke up. Be exact (to the minute) about the time. The sleep-learning process will go faster and more smoothly if you're extra careful about every little detail.

- Check in at your designated intervals, recording each one. Just as we did at bedtime, we're giving your child a little bit of space and time so she can put herself back to sleep. Remember, stay calm and loving as you support her, but stay 30 seconds or less. (In between checks, if it's not too late, call your parents and tell them how much you appreciate them now that you're a mom or dad going through all of this!) Keep checking at your designated intervals and record when your child falls asleep. You'll now want to tally up how long that particular wake-up lasted.

Each time your child awakens during the night, respond in exactly this same way, at your designated intervals. Record each check-in as well as the total amount of time it took for your child to go to sleep each time.

For Bed Sleepers Using a Safety Gate

- If you did not need to close the gate at bedtime (because your child stayed in bed) but he has gotten out of bed now, simply walk your child back to his room and say, "Good night, honey. I'll close the gate now to keep you safe." Then leave the room.

- Follow the instructions above for crib sleepers. Remember not to allow your verbal child to entangle you in middle-of-the-night negotiations.

Changing Diapers in the Middle of the Night

Try not to change your child's diaper in the middle of the night unless it's leaking or she's pooped. Changing her diaper could bring her into a more alert state and cause her to have trouble falling back asleep. If your child is prone to diaper rash, however, feel free to change her quickly after you wake her for a feeding or during a check-in, then put her right back in her crib.

For Bed Sleepers Not Using a Safety Gate

If your child has appeared at your bedside, calmly walk him back to his bed. Continue to walk him back each time he gets up, no matter how many times this happens. Try to keep interaction or talking to an absolute minimum so as not to reinforce the wakings. Try to steady yourself and get some rest. Your child now has another good practice session under his belt.

Good Morning!

To avoid early-morning wakings, do not allow your child to get out of his crib or room until at least 11 hours after his bedtime (you can settle for

10½ hours if your child consistently—after three or more days in a row—seems rested after this much sleep). One of the most difficult times for your child to put himself back to sleep is in the early morning, particularly if he's been used to getting up or coming into bed with you at that hour. But if you get your child up too early, he's robbed of enough sleep and will start his day overtired and cranky—and will have a tougher time napping well. For additional information on how to troubleshoot early-morning wakings, please see the section entitled "Bumps in the Road" in Chapter 10, "Special Situations."

For Crib Sleepers

If your child wakes in the early-morning hours, continue to do your check-ins just as you did at bedtime and throughout the night. If he hasn't gone back to sleep, once the clock reaches your designated wake time, go into your child's room, open the blinds or turn on the light, and say, "You did it! You stayed in your crib the whole night until the sun was nice and bright! We're so proud of you!" Cuddle and hug him and give him a nice full feed, if he's ready. Whatever you do, *don't* allow your child to fall back asleep—in your arms, in your bed, or in his crib; he's spent the night practicing how to sleep on his own, and you don't want to undo your hard work.

If your child has woken early but managed to put himself back to sleep—and is still sleeping at the designated wake time—lucky you! Allow him to sleep as long as he likes, up to 12 hours; you'll want to wake him at this point to preserve his ability to nap well. If your child sleeps later than your scheduled wake time, remember to adjust his nap time later as well (but don't adjust it any earlier, to avoid a too-early schedule for the day).

For Bed Sleepers Using a Safety Gate

Follow the instructions above for crib sleepers. If the early morning is the first time your child has gotten out of bed, walk her back, close the gate, and continue to do check-ins at the gate until your designated wake time or until she goes back to sleep.

For Bed Sleepers Not Using a Safety Gate

You've Earned Bragging Rights!

Brag about your verbal child's hard work on sleep to everyone you know, with your child present—Grandma, teachers, the grocery checker, whoever is willing to listen. Your child will feel very good about her accomplishments and take great pride in her progress.

Early mornings are often extremely challenging for bed sleepers who have the freedom to leave their rooms. Your child will likely come to your room and wake you when he feels ready to get up; simply walk him back to bed, repeatedly, until the designated wake-up time. Be prepared for *plenty* of protesting at this hour, as your child will likely have a hard time going back to sleep initially. Try to keep talk and interaction to a minimum, though it may help to remind him that it's not time to get up until the sun is nice and bright (or until Mom or Dad come to get him). For these children, early-morning wakings can take up to two weeks to resolve completely, so remember to stay consistent.

Continuing to Work on Sleep

After you've made it through your first night, you're well on your way toward getting great sleep. *Hang in there*—night two can still feel a bit bumpy as your child continues to learn and adjust to all the changes. If you can manage to stay rock-solid consistent for the first few nights, though, you should see significant improvement by the third or fourth night. Often, night-sleep problems are completely resolved at this point; the only time you'll be waking up is to feed your child (if you're weaning).

It is critical, even after your child begins to solidify her skills and sleep well, not to deviate from your plan. If she should return to her old habits a couple of nights into the process after seeming to make some progress, don't panic. If you can safely rule out illness, teething, or hitting a new developmental milestone (see the developmental chapter appropriate for your child's age and also Chapter 10, "Special Situations"), just continue to respond to her using the steps outlined in this chapter. Sometimes children experience what's called an *extinction burst* a few days into the sleep-learning process, temporarily waking again throughout the night even after having learned how to sleep better. Just stay consistent with your response; usually, your child will return to good sleep again the next night.

Continue to follow the steps we've outlined until your child is sleeping well. If you're consistent, you should get great sleep at night after only a few nights.

Using a Sticker Chart

Verbal children older than age 3 can benefit from added incentives to sleep well. With poster board, make a chart called "(Insert Child's Name)'s Sleep Rules." Keep it simple; include only four rules, such as brushing teeth, putting on pj's, reading a story, and staying in bed all night. (Staying in bed all night should always be one of the rules.) Take your child to the store and let him pick out some fun stickers. Then, when he gets three of any sticker (make it easy for him to get the first three), allow him to choose a small treat from a "goodie bag" or "treasure chest" in the morning. When he gets one of the "stay in bed" stickers, up the ante a bit; offer special time with you or making cookies, for example. When he gets four "stay in bed" stickers, give him the mother lode—a trip to the zoo or the ice cream shop, or a special toy he's been wanting. The key to success with stickers charts is to explain rules *clearly* and make the reward as immediate as possible (in other words, don't save the goodie bag for bedtime the next night). When your child has been sleeping well for a week or so, you can fade the rewards.

A Few Last Words

If you feel like you haven't made progress with your child's sleep in more than four days—in other words, you've hit a plateau, or you feel like you're regressing—reread this chapter and Chapter 2, "Creating Your Child's Custom Sleep Plan," *carefully* to make sure you haven't missed an important detail (such as putting your child down awake or setting an appropriate bedtime). If you still have questions or want additional support, read the developmental chapter appropriate to your child's age and Chapter 10, "Special Situations," which contains all of the information we provide to our clients as we're working together and questions come up.

CHAPTER FOUR

The Truth About Crying: Supporting Your Child While He Learns to Sleep

D eciding when and how to support your child is arguably the most critical component of any sleep plan, given that children will cry more or less, and for longer or shorter periods, depending on what you do to help them as they learn. As you probably already know, this is the aspect of sleep learning that is the most hotly debated and is also the one that tends to push parents' emotional buttons. Remember, no matter what you do to help your child sleep, *some crying is inevitable* as your child feels frustrated in her learning process and hasn't yet learned how to soothe herself. What's also inevitable, though, is that *you* feel uneasy about moving forward and making changes with your child's sleep, and we understand why. When we work with families, there is always a point in our meeting together when we need to explore the emotional side of helping a child learn how to sleep, and we'd like to do the same for you now.

When you begin teaching your child to sleep, it's normal to feel pulled in two different directions. On the one hand, you know your child and family need to sleep better, and you know you need to make changes, but on the other hand, you're more than a little reluctant to move forward with your plan. In other words, your head and heart are at war (we're guessing that's about 99.9 percent of you). If you're like most of our clients, you may be thinking one or more of the following:

- We know our child and family need better sleep, but we're *terrified* to start this process. Will he still know we love him? Will he hate us in the morning?

- Letting my child cry seems so cruel. Is this really okay?

- My young child will scream if I don't lie down with her. I just can't take the bedtime battles anymore, but I feel terrible telling her to go to sleep by herself!

Having these concerns and mixed feelings is normal. Honestly, we'd be worried about you if you didn't share some of them; your attentiveness to your child's well-being indicates that you're a caring, loving parent. And besides, who likes to listen to their child cry?

Why Do Children Cry as
They Learn How to Sleep?

It would be nice if your child could learn how to sleep without any crying or frustration whatsoever. Almost any parent would sign up for that. Unfortunately, the reality is that all children, regardless of the method you use to help them sleep, inevitably do shed tears in the process. Let's talk for a moment about why this is so.

First and foremost, children cry when learning to sleep because they are protesting change. As any parent of a child of any age will tell you, kids hate change. Do you remember what your favorite book was as a kid? Do you remember wanting to read that book over and over and over again, even though you knew every word by heart? Do you also remember a time when your parent tried to skip a line or a paragraph or a page, in the interest of getting you to sleep a little faster? And what was your response? "*Hey! That's not how it goes! You forgot the part where the blue pony meets the green pig!*" We all resist change, children and adults alike. It's normal to do so, and it's normal for your child to express his resistance by crying.

Second, as children begin to learn how to sleep but haven't yet figured out how to do so, they are, understandably, a bit frustrated. They no longer have Mom and Dad to depend on to get to sleep, and they don't yet know what to do differently. The key word is *yet*. What's interesting about falling asleep is that although each of us is born with the inherent ability to do so, it is considered a learned behavior. And yet you can't teach anyone else how to do it; you can't say to your child, "Okay, honey, just lie down, close your eyes, and hold your body very still." Instead, each of us has to learn for ourselves what to do to settle into sleep.

Some children seem to learn how to sleep almost magically, with little or no effort on the parents' part—they sleep well from birth, or get the hang of it in the first few months, and it's smooth sailing into dreamland every night even if they are rocked or fed to sleep. That's all very well for them, but your child is different. He, along with many others, hasn't learned this important skill yet, which is why he now needs you to take a step back, so he has an opportunity to figure out how to do it. If going in and picking him up or lying down with him whenever he cried taught him how to sleep, you'd be doing that right now. Oh, wait—you *have* been doing just that, and that hasn't worked! So now, your child must figure out what *he* can do, on his own, to soothe his body into sleep.

How will he do it? Well, he might kick his legs around a bit. He might gently rock his head from side to side, or he might grab his blankie. Or maybe he'll suck on his hand if he's a baby, or a thumb. Maybe, if he's a bit older, he'll twirl his hair or hug his stuffed dinosaur. Each of us has different things we do to soothe ourselves into sleep, and your child will find the exact combination that's just perfect for him. But he won't discover those things nearly as easily with you standing right next to him or patting him or picking him up, because he won't have the motivation to do so; instead, he will expect you to give him whatever help you always have, and he will likely feel even more frustrated than he already does about why you are standing right there but *not* helping him all the way to sleep. In other words, if you "help" him by patting, hugging, or picking him up, *he will cry even harder and for longer* because the touching feels like a tease—and serves to reinforce the crying.

Can Crying Harm a Child?

There is no evidence that allowing a child to cry while parents intermittently offer support does any psychological damage whatsoever. We are social workers who have always remained heart-centered in our work. When we began to help parents with sleep learning, we worried—just like everyone else—that perhaps children would be frightened in the morning after crying during the night, avoiding their parents or showing some indication that they had been traumatized. We assure you that if we had *ever* heard feedback along these lines, we would have abandoned our practice long ago. But instead, what we hear repeatedly is that even if they do cry a bit at night, children consistently wake up happy to see Mom and Dad in the morning. They don't hold a grudge, and they don't interact any differently. (Note: children *can* seem a bit sluggish during the first few days of sleep learning, as their bodies begin to catch up on all the sleep they need.) In fact, as they begin to get better sleep over a couple of days, children begin to seem more attached than ever, because they are rested enough to be able to be fully present in their relationships with their parents (and that works both ways; as Mom and Dad begin to feel rested, too, they are more fully engaged with their child). Parents repeatedly tell us that almost immediately—with the first signs of better sleep— their children's alertness, mood, and behavior all improve dramatically. We can't even count how many times we've heard reports of children hitting a major developmental milestone *right* on the heels of learning how to sleep well, because they finally have the energy to do so.

Having now done this work for over a decade, and having helped thousands of families through the process of getting better sleep, if there were a downside to allowing a child to cry *for a few minutes at a time*, we would have come across it by now. Many of our families keep in touch with us, checking in from time to time as their children change and grow. From our experience, once families have laid a solid foundation of sleep using our methods, their relationships with their children only continue to flourish and thrive.

What is damaging to your child is when you are inconsistent in your response to her, making different choices each night—for example, sometimes allowing your child to cry, sometimes going in to pat her or pick her up—because these mixed messages will cause your child to *cry more*. That's because what you're practicing is called intermittent reinforcement, in which sometimes you encourage your child's crying behavior by picking her up or consoling her, and sometimes you ignore the behavior. Believe it or not, using intermittent reinforcement is the most surefire, guaranteed way to continue a behavior, because it encourages your child to believe that if she cries long and hard enough, you will eventually help her to sleep. The crying will go on for weeks or months, and this is when we feel it crosses the line from temporary frustration to unnecessary, intermittent neglect.

Yeah, But . . .

Even after hearing all of the reasons children learn faster and cry less when parents don't touch as they check in, sometimes parents still feel uneasy. In our practice, we call this reaction "Yeah, but . . ." You can finish the sentence in a variety of ways: What if she really needs me? What if she's scared or lonely? What if something's wrong? If you know your child isn't sick or teething, she's not in pain or discomfort. For younger babies, you've taken care of her hunger by giving her milk at bedtime and setting a weaning schedule, if appropriate. When a child cries, parents experience an automatic knee-jerk response—which is actually a biological urge—to act immediately to help their child to calm. In almost any other scenario, this response would be appropriate. But remember, you've *been* responding to her just this way, and that hasn't helped her learn how to sleep.

There are times in the course of your child's growth and development when she will be attempting to learn an important new skill, and she'll feel some frustration in the process of that learning. Take crawling as an example. When children are on the brink of learning to crawl, they often rock back and forth on their hands and knees, trying to get to a toy that's just out of reach. The baby cries and complains as she reaches out in frustration, and what's your first temptation? To scoot the toy closer, of course, so she won't have to struggle. But what has she missed if you do this? An opportunity to feel a bit of frustration . . . which then leads to an idea: "Well, maybe if I move my knee a little closer to my hand, I can reach my hand farther." Bingo! Whether your child is learning to walk, tie a shoe, ride a bike, or do math homework, each time your child struggles, it's going to be tempting to jump in and rescue her. But when you do this, you are actually preventing her from learning *for herself* what she can do to alleviate her frustration—in other words, learning the skill that will help her grow and develop as a human being.

Learning how to sleep is one of the most fundamentally important skills each human being needs to master. But to find her new skills, your child needs you to give her some time and space, which can be extremely difficult. But it's worth it, because in waiting a few minutes at a time as you check in on her, you are doing something important: you are supporting her need to sleep—and her good health.

A Few Words About Older Children

For toddlers and preschoolers, the protesting can look (and sound) a bit different. Most parents of kids this age have had some success in allowing their children to learn to self-soothe, but children will often test limits at bedtime simply because they'd rather stay up later, have some company as they go to sleep, or snuggle with you in the middle of the night. Stalling by asking for one more story, one more sip of water, or to lie down with you is common. (If your child is legitimately anxious, please read the section entitled "Fears" in Chapter 9, the developmental chapter for 2- to 5-year-olds.)

But if your child is simply testing limits, it is time for you to lovingly set clear boundaries, so he will get the sleep that's so vital to his good health. This can be harder when a child is verbal, and on top of the crying you bear witness to an all-out tantrum as he protests not getting what he's used to getting. You might hear something along the lines of, "I don't like you, Mommy," or "I promise, I'll sleep in my bed *tomorrow* night!" Some children are clever little negotiators who can seem like trial attorneys arguing their most important case. But it is critical for you to have a strong defense (infused with lots of love, of course!).

When she's been protesting consistently for months or years, trying to convince a toddler or preschooler to go to bed smoothly is no easier than trying to convince a teenager to wear the floral jumper that Grandma gave her for Christmas. So remember, as you make changes to your child's routine, she is going to respond with some disappointment (at best) or even strong anger (at worst) about your decision. This doesn't mean that your decision is wrong. It just means that your child doesn't feel happy about it. If your child is verbal, you can have lots of discussion about sleep changes before and after bedtime or nap time, which will help her not only to process the changes but also to feel proud of her accomplishments.

When your confidence wavers as you help your child learn to sleep, think about how he is when he doesn't get enough sleep at night. Don't you notice that he has a hard time regulating his emotions during the day, up one minute and down the next? Doesn't he have a harder time behaving well at school? Isn't he more likely to whine and tantrum? Once your child begins getting the rest he needs, just watch how he thrives.

Consistency Is Key

Please remember this: *consistency is the single most important factor in helping your child sleep quickly, with a minimum amount of crying.* If you sometimes hold your child and sometimes allow her to cry, your child will become extremely confused and only cry longer and harder. To get through the sleep-learning process quickly, it's important to respond to your child with one clear, consistent message.

We're With You in Spirit!

Finally, although we won't be physically standing in your bedroom holding your hand while your child learns to sleep, we want you to know that we really will be holding your hand in spirit. (And in Appendix B, "Crying 911: Emergency Help for Panicked Parents," you'll find the words of support we would offer if we were right there with you.) Our hearts, thoughts, and prayers—for speedy resolution to all of your sleep problems—will be with you every step of the way. We like to think that all the babies, toddlers, children, and families who have come before you and navigated their way to getting great sleep will be with you in spirit, too—and if *they* could do it, so can *you*. As we often say, thousands of families can't be wrong—and soon you'll be joining those ranks too!

CHAPTER FIVE

The Art of the Nap

Because there are so many variables involved with naps, and because it can take some real finessing to get them just right, we do believe there's an art to working on naps. The potential hurdles, though, are worth jumping over, as your child's ability to nap well will intricately affect her ability to sleep well at night.

Before reading this chapter, you'll want to make sure you've read Chapter 3, which explains central concepts that apply to both nighttime and daytime sleep. We usually encourage families to work on both nights and naps simultaneously so that children can practice new skills round the clock and learn all of their skills quickly.

Why Isn't My Child Napping Well?

Poorly timed naps are the most common cause of short or incon-sistent naps, largely because young children have such a small win-dow in which they are tired enough to sleep long enough but not so overtired that they wake up too early from the nap. In this section, we'll cover detailed scheduling information according to age, so feel free to skip to the section that pertains to your child.

A word of warning about naps: they are *much* harder to fix than night-time sleep, so please don't feel discouraged if you see quick and (rela-tively) easy success with your nights but find that you're struggling a bit longer with the naps. There are three main reasons why naps are tricky:

1. Kids' bodies aren't as tired as they are at nighttime after a long day, so falling asleep and staying asleep are more difficult.

2. Kids are aware that there's daylight outside, and they don't want to slow their bodies down or stop what they're doing to sleep.

3. Children love spending time with loved ones and familiar caregivers during the day, and they don't want to be apart from you, even for a little while.

Even though nap problems take a bit longer to resolve, your child *will* learn how to nap well if you follow your plan carefully. As always, consistency in how you respond to your child as she learns is key to your success.

As you help your child adjust to a new nap schedule, you'll find that she seems a bit overtired at times as she learns her new skills, perhaps not yet sleeping a full hour for each nap. Although we've warned against allowing your child to become overtired, when helping her learn how to nap well we need to help her nap at the right time and to allow her to stay awake long enough between sleep periods during the day that she can both fall asleep *and stay asleep* for at least an hour. When helping your child adjust to her new nap schedule, stretch her as close to the next sleep period as you can without allowing her to become exhausted. In general, babies under 6 months will have a harder time waiting all the way until the next nap time than will children older than 6 months.

Daytime Wake Windows

AGE	Wake Time Until 1st Nap	End of 1st Nap Until 2nd Nap	End of 2nd Nap Until 3rd Nap
0–4 months:	variable	variable	variable
4–6 months:	2 hours	2½ hours	2½ hours
6–9 months:	2–2½ hours	2½–3 hours	2½–3 hours
9–12 months:	2½–3 hours	3–3½ hours	N/A
12–18 months:	3–4 hours	3–4 hours	N/A
18–24 months:	5–6 hours	N/A	N/A
2–3 years:	6–7 hours	N/A	N/A
3–5 years:	7–8 hours *(if still napping)*		

Creating Your Child's Nap Plan:
For Your 4- to 6-Month-Old

At 4 months, your baby is ready for a sleep schedule, and she now needs to sleep 3 to 4 hours during the day. You'll determine the timing of her naps based on the morning wake time. Babies this age need three naps a day of at least 1 hour (or very close to 1 hour) in length, and they can stay awake about 2 hours between their morning wake up and first nap. So if your child sleeps from 7:00 PM to 6:00 AM, for example, her first nap will come about 2 hours after her morning waking, at 8:00 AM, and will ideally last at least an hour.

Some 4-month-old babies are not quite ready to stretch their daytime wake windows to 2 hours until closer to 4½ months. These babies may also not be able to sleep more than 45 minutes for a nap. In this case, you can allow your baby to take her first nap 1½ hours after she wakes for the day, then put her down every 2 hours for the rest of the day. In other words, your baby will probably take four naps rather than three. Once your baby is 4½ months old, though, try to stretch her the additional half hour per wake time interval to help her consolidate her nap sleep.

If your child sleeps later than 6:00 AM (or your intended wake time), you can adjust the first nap later to accommodate. In other words, if he sleeps until 6:30 AM, your child will go down for a nap 2 hours later, at 8:30, for at least 1 hour; if he sleeps until 6:45 AM, he'll nap at 8:45. However, you will *not* adjust the nap time any earlier than that 2-hour window while doing sleep learning, even if the baby wakes early and never falls back asleep; doing so will shift your schedule too early and cause the rest of the naps for the day to be mistimed. For example, if your baby's bedtime is 7:00 PM, and he woke at 5:30 AM the first day, you would still use 6:00 AM as the wake time even though he didn't fall back asleep, and the first nap would still be at 8:00 AM (not 7:30).

The second nap generally comes about 2½ hours after the *end* of the first nap. In other words, if your child sleeps from 8:00 to 9:00 AM for her first nap, her next nap would be at 11:30 AM for at least 1 hour.

The third nap then comes 2½ hours after the *end* of the second nap. So using the same example, if the second nap ended at 12:30 PM, your child would then take her third nap at 3:00 PM for at least 1 hour.

At this age, it is wise to make sure your baby is awake at least 2 to 2½ hours between the *end* of the last nap and bedtime so that he is sufficiently tired to sleep for the night—so be careful not to allow that third nap to begin or end too late. If his bedtime is 7:00 PM, for instance, make sure the baby finishes his last nap by 5:00 PM.

Sample Schedule for a 4- to 6-Month-Old:

Bedtime: 7:00 PM
Wake time: 6:00 AM
First nap: 8:00 AM (sleeps till 9:00 AM)
Second nap: 11:30 AM (sleeps till 12:30 PM)
Third nap: 3:00 PM (sleeps till 4:00 PM)

Many children will sleep longer than 1 hour for one or more of the naps, but you can still use the formula of scheduling the first nap 2 hours after the morning wake up time, scheduling the second nap 2½ hours after the end of the first nap, and scheduling the third nap 2½ hours after the end of the second nap. You can use the third nap as a kind of balance for your total amount of day sleep, which means that sometimes this nap can be very short, or what we call a "blip" nap of perhaps only 30 to 45 minutes. In other words, if your child slept 90 minutes for the first nap and 75 minutes for the second nap, he'd already have gotten 2¾ hours of day sleep, very close to the minimum of 3 hours. In this case, if he took only a 45-minute third nap, that would be fine.

Here's another sample schedule for 4- to 6-month-old; in this case, the baby naps longer than 1 hour for her first and second naps.

Bedtime: 7:00 PM

Wake time: 6:00 AM

First nap: 8:00 AM (sleeps till 9:30 AM)

Second nap: 12:00 PM (sleeps till 1:15 PM)

Third nap: 3:45 PM (sleeps till 4:30 PM)

Here's one more sample schedule for a 4- to 6-month-old who gets most of her daytime sleep in the first two naps:

Bedtime: 7:00 PM
Wake time: 6:00 AM
First nap: 8:00 AM (sleeps till 10:00 AM)
Second nap: 12:30 PM (sleeps till 1:30 PM)
Third nap: 4:00 PM (sleeps till 4:30 PM)

Remember, every child is different, and as long as your child's cumulative daytime sleep amounts to 3 to 4 hours, you're doing well.

Creating Your Child's Nap Plan: For Your 6- to 9-Month-Old

At 6 to 9 months, your baby now needs to sleep 2 to 3 hours total during the day, made up in two or three naps. While your baby is still taking three naps, he will be able to stay awake 2 hours between his wake time for the day and the start of nap one, and 2½ hours between the end of nap one and the beginning of nap two, and 2½ hours from the end of nap two to the beginning of nap three.

Here's a sample schedule for a child 6 to 9 months old:

Bedtime: 7:00 PM
Wake time: 6:00 AM
First nap: 8:00 AM (sleeps till 10:00 AM)
Second nap: 12:30 PM (sleeps till 1:30 PM)
Third nap: 4:00 PM (sleeps till 4:15 PM)

Transitioning from Three Naps to Two Naps

This is the age range during which your baby will transition from three to two naps; the third nap will continue to shrink slowly (sometimes lasting only a 10- or 15-minute "blip") until it disappears altogether. Gradually, your child will begin to resist taking the third nap entirely; when she refuses this nap consistently for four to six days in a row, she is ready to drop the nap. Warning: you will then enter what we fondly call the "Yuck Zone," where three naps seem like too many but two naps don't seem like enough. On some days your child may still need a very short third "blip" nap (often in the car or stroller), and on other days two longer naps will seem sufficient. The key is to follow her lead, allowing for a bit more flexibility with naps until she has fully transitioned to two naps (this usually takes one to two weeks).

When your child transitions from three naps to two naps, you'll need to adjust her daytime wake windows later by 30 minutes each, so that the first nap is scheduled 2½ hours after wake time and the second nap is scheduled 3 hours after the end of the first nap. So if your child wakes at 6:30 AM, move the first nap to 9:00 AM. If she sleeps an hour, the second nap will now occur at 1:00 PM.

Sample Schedule for Two Naps a Day

Bedtime: 7:30 PM

Wake time: 6:30 AM

First nap: 9:00 AM (sleeps till 10:00 AM)

Second nap: 1:00 PM (sleeps till 2:30 PM)

When your child first begins to transition from three to two naps, you'll temporarily need to adjust the bedtime earlier—by a half hour to as much as 1 hour—to help your child avoid becoming overtired; try to be careful, though, that your bedtime doesn't become so early that her wake time also shifts earlier (as long as you don't adjust by more than 1 hour, you should be okay). The earliest we usually recommend shifting bedtime is to about 6:30 PM.

Your Child's Nap Plan: For Your 9- to 12-Month-Old

Pre-toddlerhood is a time when children are generally steady on two naps a day, and parents can feel free to coast a bit. What may happen, however, is that children this age begin to resist either their morning or afternoon nap, fooling many parents into thinking that it's time to transition to one nap a day. Not quite! We find that almost all children make this shift after their

first birthday, but those who attempt to nap only once a day too
young quickly become exhausted (and have terrible night wakings
due to being overtired). A child who begins to protest her two-nap
schedule is, however, able to stay awake longer during the day, in
slow but steady increments.

Typical Schedule for a 9- to 12-Month-Old

Bedtime: 7:30 PM
Wake time: 6:30 AM
First nap: 9:00 AM (sleeps till 11:00 AM)
Second nap: 2:00 PM (sleeps till 3:00 PM)

Let's say a child on this schedule begins to protest taking her 2:00
PM nap, playing or talking in her crib until 2:30. Is she ready for one
nap? Nope! Ready to push naps later? Yes! So we would advise moving *both naps* later by half-hour increments.

Adjusting Both Naps a Half Hour Later

Bedtime: 7:30 PM
Wake time: 6:30 AM
First nap: 9:30 AM (sleeps till 11:30 AM)
Second nap: 2:30 PM (sleeps till 3:30 PM)

Your Child's Nap Plan:
For Your 12- to 24-Month-Old

Starting at 12 months, most children will nap for a total of $1^1/_2$ to 3 hours, usually made up in two naps, and can stay awake 3 to $3^1/_2$ hours in the morning before their first nap, then $3^1/_2$ to 4 hours between the end of the first nap and the beginning of the second. Then, as children grow older, they can stretch out their wakeful periods gradually, usually by 15- to 30-minute increments at a time. For guidelines according to age, refer back to the table "Daytime Wake Windows"

If your 12- to 18-month-old child is taking one nap a day, follow the guidelines for 18 to 24 months.

at the beginning of this chapter (but continue to monitor your child for individual variation).

The key is to watch your child closely and follow his lead; rather than making a decision to move his nap time later, let him show you it's time—watch for a pattern (three to four days in a row) of resistance to going down for a nap (make sure to rule out illness, teething, major separation anxiety, or a new developmental milestone). Resistance can take the form of talking or singing as your child lies in his crib, crying hard when he hasn't usually done so, or suddenly taking very short naps. When you see these signs, it's time to shift the nap time later.

If your child still protests naps after shifting the timing a half hour later, or if another few weeks goes by and he begins to have a hard time settling again, you'll need to adjust his naps later by another half hour.

Continuing to Adjust Naps Later

Bedtime: 7:30 PM

Wake time: 6:30 AM

First nap: 10:00 AM (sleeps till 11:30 AM)

Second nap: 3:00 PM (sleeps till 4:00 PM)

Beware of the Too-Late Nap!

If your child's second nap is getting so close to bedtime that he has a hard time settling to sleep on time, it's time to make the transition to one nap. Children should be awake from their nap at least 3 to 3 1/2 hours prior to bedtime at this age. If bedtime is 7:30 PM, for instance, make sure your child finishes sleeping by 4:00 or 4:30 PM.

Transitioning from Two Naps to One Nap

Children usually make this transition at about 14 to 16 months, although the range is 12 to 20 months. Once a child is unwilling or unable to take her second nap consistently for four to six days in a row, or the second nap is beginning to interfere with her ability to fall asleep at the usual bedtime, it's time to transition to one nap. That's right, you are now entering into another "Yuck Zone," where your child will resist her second nap but won't seem rested enough with only one. On some days, your child may still need a second short "blip" nap, and on other days one nap will suffice. It's a bit crazy-making as your child bounces back and forth, but usually this lasts about a month at the most.

When shifting from two naps to one, your child will still sleep a total of $1^{1}/_{2}$ to 3 hours, and you'll need to help him stretch his daytime wake window far enough in the morning that you won't have too much time "hanging" between the end of the nap and bedtime. Eventually, you're shooting for roughly a midpoint in your child's day, so there are approximately equal amounts of time between wake time in the morning and the start of the nap, and the end of the nap and bedtime. Initially, however, you may need to start out at 11:30 AM; if your child has been napping at 10:30 AM, stretch him slowly, in 15-minute increments over a period of several days to 11:30 AM.

Here are some tried-and-true tips for transitioning to one nap:

- When she first moves to one nap, your child may have trouble sleeping more than an hour, or longer than the length of her previous first nap. If this happens, try to keep her in the crib for a bit longer after she wakes, perhaps an additional 15 or 30 minutes, so she has the opportunity to go back to sleep. Do some check-ins if you need to.
  If she is not crying, you may want to leave her even longer.

- Be patient; this transition takes time, and it may be a couple of weeks until your child can nap at least $1^{1}/_{2}$ hours consistently.

- As with the transition from three to two naps, you may want to adjust the bedtime earlier temporarily; you can also try for a very short late-afternoon nap, perhaps in the stroller or car, to help tide her over till bedtime. Try to be careful, though, that your bedtime doesn't become so early that her wake time also shifts earlier (as long as you don't adjust by more than 1 hour, you should be okay).

Typical Schedule for Transitioning to One Nap

Bedtime: 7:30 PM

Wake time: 6:30 AM

Nap: 11:30 AM (sleeps till 1:30 PM)

As your child gets older, naps generally stay the same length, but your child will continue to increase his ability to stay awake longer before the nap. So a child who slept from 11:30 to 1:30 will eventually be able to nap from 12:00 to 2:00, then 12:30 to 2:30, and so on.

Sample Schedule for One Later Nap

Bedtime: 7:30 PM

Wake time: 6:30 AM

Nap: 12:00 PM (sleeps till 2:00 PM)

For Your 2- to 3-Year-Old

By age 2, most children can nap at 12:30 or 1:00 and sleep for $1\frac{1}{2}$ to 3 hours. They will need to be awake at least 4 hours prior to bedtime.

Sample Schedule for a 2-Year-Old

Bedtime: 7:30 PM
Wake time: 6:30 AM
Nap: 12:30 PM (sleeps till 2:30 PM)

Most children start to give up their nap somewhere between 3 and 4 years. However, your child may continue to nap as late as age 5 (if you're lucky!). The nap at 3 years may get even later, pushing toward 1:00 or 2:00 PM and ending around 3:30 or so.

Sample Schedule for a 3-Year-Old

Bedtime: 7:30 PM
Wake time: 6:30 AM
Nap: 1:30 PM (sleeps till 3:00 PM)

When children begin to transition from one nap to none, you'll enter the last "Yuck Zone" where your child will vacillate between needing and refusing a nap. For a while, you can follow her lead: when she does nap, maintain the bedtime as usual. If she refuses the nap, however, you'll need to put her to bed unusually early (by as much as 1 hour, if necessary). You can "cheat" by driving for the nap for a little while if the car puts her to sleep. Eventually, she'll give up the nap entirely and her body will be able to stay up till her usual bedtime.

On your Sleep Planner, complete your goal schedule by adding appropriate nap times for your child's age. NOTE: When you have more than one nap to plan for your child's schedule, the timing of the second and third naps will vary depending on what time your child wakes up from the previous nap. When planning your nap schedule, think of the goal times for the second and third naps as guidelines, not as set in stone.

Step-by-Step Sleep for Naps

Once you've reached your designated nap time, follow these guidelines. You'll use these same methods whether your child has never napped well or whether you're trying to elongate a short-nap habit.

For *each* nap, you'll give your child a minimum of 1 hour of practice time in the crib or bed, whether she sleeps or not. Every minute counts, so try not to give up after 50 or even 55 minutes. We've known many children who ended up falling asleep at the very last minute! If you leave your child in her room for the full hour, she'll have the good chance she needs to learn how to put herself to sleep.

For children napping once a day, you can begin to extend your child's time in the crib or bed once he begins to sleep close to an hour. For example, if he's learned how to sleep 50 minutes, try allowing him to stay in his crib or bed for 90 minutes, to help him continue to lengthen the nap. If he does not seem rested after learning how to sleep 90 minutes, continue to extend the length of the nap by 30-minute increments.

Prepare Your Sleep Station

Just as you did at nighttime, get your sleep station ready. Remember, this station is *critical* for following your plan correctly. If you forget what you're supposed to be doing and inadvertently give your child inconsistent or mixed messages, he will nap less and cry more. Also, writing down all the details throughout your child's learning process will help you see progress from one nap to the next. Noting his gradual improvement will also help you stay motivated to achieve your goals.

Remind Your Verbal Child About Sleep Changes

Before you begin your naptime routine, go over the new sleep rules again with your child and read your special sleep book (just as you did at nighttime). Remind her that she did a great job the previous night and that she's now going to practice falling asleep for the nap. Let her know that when naptime is over, she'll feel refreshed and you can play together. Being reminded of the plan will help your child to feel more empowered and thus more likely to cooperate.

Do a Mini Version of Your Bedtime Routine

Before the start of the nap, do a mini routine in the same space where your child will be sleeping, just as you do at nighttime. What you do for naps doesn't have to be the same as what you do at night, but the nap routine should be the same for each nap. Review your Sleep Planner to ensure that you've made all of the environmental changes necessary for your child to nap well.

Remember to *make sure your child does not fall asleep* under the same old conditions he's used to (such as while rocking or feeding or while you stay in the room). If your child is used to falling asleep on the breast or bottle, pull him off the minute you begin seeing the "drunken sailor" signs: heavy eyelids, slowed-down movement, losing consciousness fast. When this happens, give him a little bit of motion: "Honey-honey-honey! We can't fall asleep just yet." Crack the window, and get some fresh air in there. Allowing him to sleep even for a moment can take the edge off of his fatigue, preventing him from being able to nap at all.

Put Your Child in His Crib or Bed Awake

Just as at nighttime, put your child down awake. Say, "It's nap time, sweetie! See you in a little while." Then leave the room.

Do Your Check-Ins

At your sleep station, record the time you put your child to bed. Now you'll begin to lovingly support her while she learns how to sleep, just as you did at night.

For Crib Sleepers

Do your check-ins at the same intervals you used for nighttime, remembering not to touch your child; keep the check-ins brief, 30 seconds max; and try not to go in any sooner than the check-in interval so that your child will have enough time to put herself to sleep. If you find that the check-ins are just making your child cry harder, it's okay to stretch check-in intervals longer for naps, waiting as long as feels comfortable to you. Remember to record everything at your sleep station.

Key Points to Reduce Protest Crying

1. Wait the **exact** interval you've set for your check-ins.

2. **Don't touch** your child, which will tease her into thinking you'll help her to sleep.

3. **Use a calm, loving tone of voice** as you support her.

4. Stay just **30 seconds** maximum.

For Bed Sleepers Using a Safety Gate

If your child remains in bed but cries in protest, check on him after a few minutes and tell him you are proud of him for staying in bed. If he leaves the room, walk him back to his room, and calmly tell him you'll close the gate to help him stay safe in his room. Then follow the instructions above for crib sleepers, doing your check-ins from the hallway.

For Bed Sleepers Not Using a Gate

When your child gets out of bed, rather than doing check-ins, say matter-of-factly, "Oops, you got out of bed—let Mom (or Dad) walk you back." Put him back down, then leave the room again. Continue to walk your child back to bed each and every time he comes out of the room—which may last the whole hour as your child begins to work on naps—without talking (which is too stimulating for your child during the day and will make it harder for him to fall asleep). Remember to stay calm, as any reaction from you—even mild frustration—will only reinforce and continue the protesting.

Key Points to Reduce Protesting While Walking Your Child Back to Bed

1. **Don't allow yourself to get pulled into conversation** with your child, which will give her incentive to stay awake and cause her to protest for longer.

2. **Avoid caving in to demands** for water, a hug, and the like. You'll have already offered these during your wind-down routine.

3. **Don't express your anger or frustration to your child,** which will reinforce the behavior. If you need to take a break, allow the other parent to take over.

4. **Leave the room quickly** each time you return your child to bed.

Step 4:

Praise Your Child's Hard Work!

Whether she sleeps or not, congratulate your child for her excellent efforts at learning how to nap. Older children who understand your words will feel tremendously proud of their accomplishments!

Gauging Your Child's Nap Progress

In just a few days, your child will learn how to go right to sleep for naps without crying or protesting. As your child begins to learn how to sleep, though, she will likely fall into one of the following three categories.

SCENARIO 1: THE PROTESTOR

Your child may cry or protest the entire hour. *Don't worry!* This can happen during the first few attempts at making changes with naps. As difficult as this can be for both you and your child, remember that she is practicing learning how to sleep (or if older, learning new rules), even if she's not perfectly agreeable just yet. She'll get there soon!

Solution: If she doesn't sleep at all, get her up at the end of the hour and give her lots of praise anyway, telling her she tried hard. Hold her, cuddle her, and kiss her as much as you want. Then wait an hour (for babies under 6 months) or till the next nap time (for children older than 6 months) and try again.

SCENARIO 2: THE PENDULUM

In this scenario, your child may cry for a bit, then sleep for a bit, then cry some more—in other words, she may sleep off and on during the course of the hour. This may be common in her first couple of attempts at napping, as children may sleep just enough to take the edge off and then wake up, feeling rested enough.

Solution: Regardless of how much she's slept, if she's up at the end of the hour, get her up. If you want to try to stretch the nap a bit longer after a couple of days of working on naps, you can try to keep your child in her crib or bedroom an additional half hour, and when she wakes, pop your head in the door and say, "Still nap time sweetie. Go back to sleep!" Once you've taken your child out of her room, keep her up until the next scheduled nap time.

SCENARIO 3: THE PROCRASTINATOR

In this scenario, your child may cry for a significant portion of the hour (even 59 minutes!), then put herself to sleep. Hooray—she did it!

Solution: Let her go ahead and sleep as long as she likes, up to 2 hours from the time she *fell asleep*. After 2 hours, wake her up; if she's due for another nap, keep her up the appropriate interval of time prior to the next nap (see chart on page 87). Also, make sure that she wakes up early enough to be able to go down well at bedtime (see pages 88–89). Children napping once a day can sleep 3 hours.

Beware of the "In-Between" Cat Nap

Make sure not to let your child snooze, even momentarily, between your scheduled nap-times. Even a 5-minute "catnap" will likely destroy his ability to sleep well during the next nap.

When Will My Child Learn How to Nap?

Unfortunately, nap problems are *much* more challenging to solve than nighttime sleep problems; your child is attempting to put himself to sleep from a much more alert state than he experiences at night, and he will probably fight sleep a bit more during the day. Naps may take about a week to iron out completely—and in some cases it can take even longer, though this is less common. If your child is especially talented at fighting daytime sleep, and you've been working on naps for a week or longer, you may need to extend the crib time to 75 or 90 minutes to give your child a chance to fall asleep (or back to sleep if she's woken partway through).

Working on Naps Can Be Exhausting!

If you feel overwhelmed by all of the effort involved in improving your child's ability to nap, you're not alone! Most of the families we work with express the same sentiments. If you're finding that your child's struggles day and night are just too much for you to handle right now, and you're wondering whether you can put the naps aside for fine-tuning later, the answer is yes. Although your child won't have consistent practice in learning his new sleep skills if you separate working on nighttime and nap time sleep, the brain does organize night sleep and day sleep differently, so you can continue to enjoy success with the changes you're making at night but continue to help her to sleep during the day. If you have a child who will sleep with motion—car or stroller—these options are preferable over nursing or rocking to sleep, but if the latter are your *only* options, go ahead and use them. If you're not going to work on naps for now, do try to help your child get as much nap sleep as possible while you're working on night sleep to ensure that she isn't too overtired by bedtime (which will cause higher levels of cortisol and more crying). If your child cannot nap well no matter what you do to help her, it's best to move forward with sleep learning for naps.

The Emergency Nap

If you have tried several times in a day to help your child nap well, or if your child has gotten only fragmented nap sleep on a given day, put her in the car or stroller and allow her to take a nap (preferably of at least 1 hour) with motion. This way, she'll avoid becoming overtired by bedtime, which will make it tougher for her to fall and stay asleep. If you have the option, motion naps are preferable to using old habits (such as nursing, rocking, or lying down with your child) to help your child sleep.

CHAPTER SIX

Alternative Methods for Sleep Learning

With every family who comes to see us at Sleepy Planet, we weigh the pros and cons of various methods for teaching a child to sleep. Most parents wish to get through the process quickly with a minimum amount of crying, which is why we most often recommend the methods outlined in Chapter 3, "Step-by-Step Sleep." However, if it feels better for you to hug your child or stay in the room, follow your instincts! Just know that no matter what you do, you can never completely erase your child's frustration as she learns how to sleep; unfortunately, she will protest no matter what you do.

Some parents believe that leaving the room and not picking up their child will cause him to feel abandoned. Rest assured, there is no evidence suggesting that allowing a child to cry for a few minutes at a time, for a few days, harms a child, and we see only happy, rested children after they've come to us for help. However, you need to feel comfortable with the method you use to help your child sleep, or the method won't work. Almost all sleep methods, whether or not they involve staying in the room or touching, work for some people; the variables are the length of time the process takes and how much crying overall is involved. For instance, patting or holding your child may help him calm in the moment, but he may cry harder and longer when you leave again—and he may take several weeks versus several nights to learn how to sleep, which usually means more crying overall.

The bottom line is that you are the expert on your child, and any of the following alternatives will also help your child learn how to sleep.

If Your Child Sleeps in a Crib

There are several ways that you can modify your sleep learning plan when your child sleeps in a crib, depending on your preferences.

1. If you want a bit more contact with your child, you can go to him at the first check-in and pat him gently or hug him with some loving words of encouragement for 1 minute. After you've calmed your child, tell him, "Go night-night, honey, Mommy is right nearby," and leave the room, checking in again at your second and third intervals using the same methods.

2. Another alternative is to sit on a chair near your child's crib or lie on the floor near the crib without touching him. We often encourage this method if a parent feels concerned about potential separation anxiety, as you can remove the

element of separation by staying nearby while continuing to hold your ground. Warning: many parents who try using this method find it very difficult to watch their upset child at close range without being able to soothe her. Seeing you so close by, your little one will likely have a much harder time calming, as she will expect you to go to her and do whatever you usually do to help her.

If Your Child Sleeps in a Bed

Many parents feel that in encouraging their child to sleep more independently, he will feel afraid, suffering alone in his room. Before you begin to work on sleep, if you've assessed that your child is not afraid of his room, the dark, or monsters and that he isn't experiencing a bout of separation anxiety, then his protest behavior is usually due to limit testing. The best way to stop testing behaviors is to remain loving and calm but not to pay much attention to them and not to feed a tantrum by engaging with your child. Here are some alternatives to help your child sleep:

1. If encouraging your child to sleep in her room by herself feels like too big of a leap, you can set up a bed for yourself on the floor of your child's room (but do very little interacting), and at your designated intervals tell her, "Go to sleep, sweetie . . . I'm here." If she pops out of bed, calmly help her back to bed each time.

2. Some parents use the gate as a boundary so their child won't continue to leave the room but opt to sleep outside on an air mattress in the hallway for a couple of nights until he becomes more proficient at sleeping.

Avoid the Extended Campout

If you decide to sleep in your child's room or nearby, we recommend staying for only about two to three nights. If you stay much longer, you may be creating a new association that could be tough to break.

We've seen the toughest business executive by day opt for this choice at night, snoozing all night long in her child's Cinderella sleeping bag right outside of the room. (Imagine how much you'll appreciate your own bed once you finally return!) If you need to do check-ins, do them from your hallway bed. It's best not to enter into the room once you've positioned yourself in the hallway. Know that you are supporting your child's learning with your physical presence—and that should be enough without getting into negotiation with your child, as you may have done in the past.

Cosleeping (Also Known As "The Family Bed")

Whether families choose to cosleep or have their children sleep independently is a very personal decision, and if both parents and child are safe, rested, and fulfilled, we fully support a family's decision to share a bed. If you are committed to cosleeping, it is still possible for you to use the methods outlined in this book to get great sleep, with a few modifications. Remember also that your resolve in staying consistent with your child in the middle of the night can be a bit trickier when you are cosleeping.

You can still encourage a proper sleep and feeding schedule for your child if he is bed sharing and keep up a predictable routine around sleep. Doing so will also help to protect him against becoming overtired, which will wreak havoc on the quantity and quality of sleep for all.

Deciding to Cosleep

Making a commitment to the family bed requires some very careful thinking about what you and your spouse feel is right for you as individuals, as a couple, and as a family. If you are thinking about sharing a bed or are already doing so, ask yourselves the following questions:

1. Is it nice to think about enjoying the coziness of sleeping in close proximity, or does one or more of us tend to stay active during sleep (potentially disrupting the others)?

2. Does everyone in our family want to cosleep, or are we leaning toward cosleeping because one of us feels strongly? If one family member is sleeping in another space instead of in the family bed (for example, to sleep more soundly), are we okay with that arrangement?

3. Are we willing to commit to being quiet after our child falls asleep, or do we like to watch TV or talk in bed? (If the latter, consider using headphones, and plan some time, at least a couple of times a week, for adult conversation.)

4. Are we agreeable to getting into bed when our child does, to ensure his safety? Can we think of creative ways to connect as a couple at other times of the day?

5. Will we enjoy being able to feed our baby more often throughout the night, or will having her next to us make it tougher to wean nighttime feeds?

6. For working parents, does sleeping next to our child allow us to feel more connected to him, and him to us?

Write a list of any additional questions together, spend some time discussing your answers, and really think this decision through.

If you and your spouse would like to cosleep, try to figure out the safest way in which to do so. (Please see page 126 in Chapter 7 for the American Academy of Pediatrics' most recent guidelines for prevention against sudden infant death syndrome [SIDS] and cosleeping if you have a baby under 12 months.)

SIDS and Your Child's Safety

The American Academy of Pediatrics advises parents of babies under 12 months not to cosleep but to have babies sleep *near* parents in a crib or attachable "cosleeper." They note that SIDS risk decreases when babies sleep in their own space but in close proximity to parents, because babies are protected from suffocation by pillows or heavy blankets, are less likely to be at risk of another body rolling onto them, and have greater ability, if sleeping face down, to access adequate air.

A Middle-of-the-Road Option

We'd like to point out that attachment can be achieved between parents and children in *several* ways. If you find that cosleeping presents some challenges for you, a nice middle-of-the-road option might be keeping your child in your room but placing her in a "cosleeper" that attaches to your bed or in her own crib. (A common age at which parents choose to transition babies out of the family bed to their own sleep space is 3 to 4 months. For help with transitioning your child from your bed to hers, see Chapter 10, "Special Situations.")

Keeping Your Child's Crib in Your Room

It's no problem to keep your child nearby for now, then transition her to her own room later, when you're ready. Simply follow the steps outlined in Chapter 3 with a few modifications:

- When it's time to do the bedtime routine, go into your room. If you normally dress and change your child in her own room, try to move whatever you need into your own room so that you can do the entire bedtime routine in there.

- When doing check-ins in the middle of the night, you can stay in your bed if the crib is nearby, and do your checks from there; if the crib is more than a couple of feet away, you can get out of bed to do the check-ins, but return to your own bed while you wait between intervals.

- If you are feeding or weaning feeds in the middle of the night, get your child out of her crib and feed her on a chair in your room.

We've noticed that parents who share a room with their child often experience more early-morning wakings; your child, in a lighter sleep phase at the end of her night, becomes aware of your presence in the room and wakes, excited to begin her day with you. If you need to do check-ins with her at an early-morning hour, be sure not to make eye contact or interact with her between your check-ins. Room-darkening shades will also help prevent her propensity to wake earlier than she should. Beware that when sharing a room, early-morning wakings can take several weeks to iron out completely (though your child's sleep will improve vastly in other areas).

Step-by-Step Sleep for Cosleeping Families

Step 1:

Create a Safe Sleeping Environment

- Safety proof your bed and the perimeter around it. Children who are mobile could be in danger in a bed that is high off of the floor. Lower your bed to the ground by removing the frame and storing it elsewhere. Pad the floor around you with soft cushions or pillows in case your child falls.

Nurturing Your Relationship— and Yourself—While Cosleeping

If you and your spouse do decide to cosleep, talk about finding a way to maintain some intimate time even though your child sleeps in bed with you. You may need to find another place in your home in which to connect physically. Also, make sure you each get some free time to yourselves. Doing so will help you to rejuvenate and feel balanced as you continue to bed share for the long haul.

- Once your child is crawling, baby-proof your entire room so she cannot get hurt should she decide to do a little nighttime exploring.

- If your child is under 6 months old, position all pillows and blankets away from her body to avoid suffocation or airway obstruction.

- If you are taking medications or drinking alcohol, it may be unwise to cosleep, as you may not be able to stay alert enough to your baby's safety.

- Smoking in close proximity to a baby should be strictly avoided as doing so greatly increases SIDS risk. Create a smoke-free zone for your baby, and if you or your family members smoke, do so outside and away from the baby.

- Do not allow older siblings to sleep near a young baby in bed, as doing so raises the risk of suffocation tremendously.

Wean Nighttime Feeds (if Appropriate)

While weaning nighttime feeds, get out of bed and sit in a nearby chair or rocker so you will be able to pay careful attention to the amount of milk you are giving your child, and so you don't fall asleep accidentally and overfeed. Make sure to set your alarm for the designated times you need to wean, even though your child is lying right beside you and may wake up from the alarm. While in bed with your child, you might want to wear a tight tank top to prevent your child from having easy access to milk (and from smelling the milk).

Step 3:

Put Your Child Down Awake and Offer Support While He Learns

Be sure to read Chapter 3 to glean information about the importance of consistency and how to handle early-morning wakings.

For Babies

Try not to touch your child as he is attempting to soothe himself to sleep. With him right next to you, it will be extremely tempting to reach over and give him a big, giant hug. But try to restrain from too much touching, or the crying will go on much longer than it needs to. Keep a digital clock nearby, and say a few soothing words to your child every few minutes (plan these intervals in advance). Continue to soothe him this way until he falls asleep, and again if he wakes before your designated wake time (unless you are scheduled to feed). Alternatively, if you feel you must touch your child, pat him while he works on getting himself back to sleep, but note that doing so may make him cry harder and longer. Remember that you are lying there right beside your child, and his crying has more to do with frustration than anything else. He'll learn how to sleep quickly if you stay consistent with your soothing method. Record your check-ins on paper or on your Sleep Chart (go to www.sleepy-planet.com, under "Tips & Tools").

For Toddlers and Preschoolers

- Tell your child that although your family loves sleeping together, his night waking (or early-morning rising) isn't good for any of you. Explain that there are some new rules at bedtime. Tell him that when he wakes, Mommy and Daddy will be lying right near him but will not talk and will not play until the sun is nice and bright. There won't be any more milk or stories once it's time for bed. If you've made a special sleep book, read it at bedtime on the first night you begin making changes (see page 32 for instructions).

- You may need to close your door or even lock it (while you are inside the room with him), so your child can't wander through the house when he wakes at inappropriate times. As long as you are in the room with him, the closed door won't feel scary to him and will help to contain him in your room.

- If your child is apt to get up and walk around the room, install a night-light so he won't trip and fall on anything.

- Follow the instructions above for helping babies to sleep. Wean any nighttime feeds (see page 119), as your child will no longer need middle-of-the-night milk at this age. If your child wakes in the night, don't get up and follow him around the room or try to pull him back into bed. If your bed is low enough to the floor, he should be able to climb back in on his own. Just continue to do checks verbally, offering support and encouragement, at your designated intervals, staying calm and quiet between checks. He'll eventually decide it's more fun to be in bed with you. When your child protests, stay calm and avoid negotiating so as not to inadvertently reinforce the bedtime resistance or wakings.

CHAPTER SEVEN

Developmental Issues and How They Affect Sleep: Birth to Twelve Months

Welcome to parenthood! The first year of a baby's life is a time of tremendous change for everyone in the family. These twelve months can be both exciting and challenging, as babies learn how to communicate their needs and parents learn how meet them. Having a better understanding of what your baby's needs are, and how they relate to sleep, will help you navigate the twists and turns of babyhood as smoothly as possible.

Because it can be tricky to keep up with your baby's development from one month to the next—and to keep her on track with sleeping well—in this chapter we're going to discuss developmental changes according to age range. When you create your

Sleep Plan and begin to help your child sleep well, you'll want to incorporate the information presented here to make sure that you're addressing her sleep issues appropriately.

The First 4 Months

The stork just dropped off your little bundle of joy, and there is a whirlwind of activity in your home right now. For better or worse, some of the chaos is, for the time being, inevitable. The time between birth and 4 months is often called "the fourth trimester" because your baby is adapting from having all of her needs met in the womb to figuring out how to regulate her needs in the world with your help. She does this by communicating with you—with her voice (such as by crying urgently when she's hungry), with her body language (like when she folds into your arms after some playtime, showing you she's sleepy), and with her gaze (newborns can't focus very well, but you can tell when she's alert and engaged, and when she's not interested). At this age, your baby's biological and neurological systems are still underdeveloped, and she is completely dependent on you to meet all of her needs.

As for baby's sleep, there is an extremely wide range of what's considered normal at this age. Some babies sleep round the clock and never really wake up unless they want to eat; others are much more wakeful, sleeping in short bursts at night, waking to feed often, and taking short "catnaps" throughout the day. Despite what you may hear from well-meaning friends that you should get your child into a scheduled routine, *follow your child's lead*, and allow her to sleep when she wants to sleep and feed when she wants to feed. She needs you to respond to her signals during this stage, because your response is what helps her learn how to communicate to get her needs met when she's older and what helps give her the confidence at that point to meet them more independently.

If your baby's sleep is terribly erratic at this stage, hang in there. It's exhausting and overwhelming, we know. Don't be proud about reaching out for help right now—from family, friends, neighbors—or hire help if you can. The good news: after your baby reaches 4 months and 14 pounds (adjusting for any prematurity), either her sleep patterns will begin to stabilize on their own *or* you'll be able to help her at that point, because she'll be developmentally ready to learn how to sleep better. (More on this in the "Sleep Month-by-Month" section later in this chapter.)

If your baby simply won't sleep well without your help before 4 months, don't worry. There are *no bad habits* at this age; your baby legitimately needs your help, so feel free to rock, feed, bounce, or walk her to sleep. We've met some very creative parents over the years, and we've heard every trick in the book: putting the baby on top of the dryer in her carrier (closely supervised, of course), watching fish in a fish tank for hours on end—we even met one baby who would not sleep anywhere else but on the purple rug in the bathroom!

It's a myth that you need to get your baby on a strict schedule from the get-go, and doing so may actually be dangerous because her body may not be developmentally ready to wait several hours between feeds or sleep periods. For calming your baby and helping her to sleep well in the first 4 months, we highly recommend Dr. Harvey Karp's *The Happiest Baby on*

Don't Rush It

Many babies under 4 months aren't capable of sleeping in long stretches, so don't worry about bouncing, rocking, or feeding your baby to sleep. Not all babies have the ability to self-soothe at this age, so it's important *not* to do sleep learning yet or to let them cry.

the Block book and DVD; Dr. Karp suggests a variety of excellent ideas that are gentle, natural, and safe for your baby.

Take advantage of your baby's portability at this age. Many babies like to fall asleep in their carriers, in the car, or in a stroller, and will sleep just about anytime, anywhere—in a restaurant, at the movies, at a friend or family member's house. So do whatever activities are enjoyable to you, and bring the baby along with you. Her ability to sleep well "on the go" will change significantly at 4 months, when she'll need to begin getting better quality sleep in a quiet, darker environment and to have some predictability to the timing of her sleep. So enjoy the flexibility while you can.

SIDS Prevention Recommendations

Here are some of the most important recommendations from the American Academy of Pediatrics to ensure your baby's safety and well-being during sleep:

- Back to sleep: Infants should be placed in a supine (wholly on back position) for every sleep.

- Use a firm sleep surface: A firm crib mattress, covered by a sheet, is the recommended sleeping surface.

- Keep soft objects and loose bedding out of the crib: Pillows, quilts, comforters, sheepskins, stuffed toys, and other soft objects should be kept out of an infant's sleeping environment.

- Don't smoke during pregnancy: Also avoiding an infant's exposure to second-hand smoke is advisable for numerous reasons in addition to SIDS risk. *(continues)*

- A separate but proximate sleeping environment is recommended, such as a separate crib in the parent's bedroom. Bed sharing during sleep is not recommended.

- Consider offering a pacifier at nap time and bedtime: The pacifier should be used when placing infant down for sleep and not be reinserted once the infant falls asleep.

- Avoid overheating: The infant should be lightly clothed for sleep, and the bedroom temperature should be kept comfortable for a lightly clothed adult.

- Avoid commercial devices marketed to reduce the risk of SIDS: Although various devices have been developed to maintain sleep position or reduce the risk of rebreathing, none have been tested sufficiently to show efficacy or safety.

So If My Baby Isn't Sleeping, I'm Stuck?

Yes and no. If you have a baby whose sleep is extremely erratic, you'll need to wait until 4 months and 14 pounds to do intensive sleep learning. Why? Because their brains are still underdeveloped at this age, babies aren't necessarily able to do a lot of self-soothing, and it isn't fair to ask a baby to do something that she isn't yet developmentally able to do. Babies do undergo an enormous cognitive growth spurt at 3 to 4 months, however, and at this age they do then have the ability to self-soothe consistently, to learn how to fall and stay asleep, and to remember these skills from one night to the next. At 4 months, as long as the baby weighs 14 pounds and you've gotten the green light from your doctor to do sleep learning (remember to adjust for prematurity), it's perfectly fine to help your baby to learn how to put herself to sleep, and if you follow our methods, your baby will be sleeping much better in less than five nights.

Until then, there are a few things you can do to get the best sleep you can and to set the stage for good sleep later. Here's how.

Don't Overstimulate

If you need to feed or change your baby at night, try to keep the lights low and your interactions to a minimum, so you won't reinforce your baby's wakefulness by making it fun for her to see you in the middle of the night. This can be harder than it sounds. Even though you may be exhausted, the middle of the night can be a very peaceful time, and the baby looks so adorable as she's gazing up at you lovingly (that is, if you're able to hold your own eyes open at this hour!). Nonetheless, if your habit is to coo and chitchat with her, as she gets older she'll begin to understand that this is playtime for the two of you and may wake in anticipation of getting to see you.

Get into a Routine

At about 8 weeks, you can begin using a bedtime routine. A bed-time routine is a series of predictable events that help a baby to unwind at day's end and help her understand that it's time to sleep. At this age, it won't take much; a bath (if you wish), some rocking and/or singing, and a feed will probably do the trick. You will prob-ably rock or feed your baby to sleep as the last part of the routine— and that's just fine! (Remember, there are *no bad habits* right now.)

As the baby gets older (4 months and beyond), your routine may expand to include other activities, too, like a massage, a book, or some quiet play on the floor. It doesn't really matter what you choose to do in your routine—as long as you keep an eye toward slowing things down—but what does matter is that you do the same things every night in the same order,

in the space where your baby sleeps,
so she can relax her body in that
room. If you relax and feed her in
your cozy living room and then
whisk her away to a dark bedroom,
she may feel justly unhappy about
the abrupt change in location just
before sliding off into dreamland.

Use a Bedtime Routine as Early as 8 Weeks

A bedtime routine will help your baby understand that sleep is coming and help her wind her body down after a day filled with stimulation and activity.

Put Your Baby Down Drowsy but Awake

Closer to 3 months, if your
baby isn't sleeping well at night or during the day, you can begin to
experiment with putting her down drowsy but increasingly awake.
(Please note that babies' night sleep will begin to smooth out before
the naps do. It's wise to begin this experiment with the nighttime
first and then work on the daytime sleep.) If you usually feed her to
sleep, you can gently unlatch her from the breast or bottle as she
begins to get sleepy but *before* she actually falls asleep. Try to put her
down, but stay nearby. If she begins to fuss, try to soothe her by using
your voice to reassure her, singing, or patting or rubbing her tummy
gently. If she begins to cry in earnest, pick her up and calm her, then
try again to put her down. Initially, you might need to repeat this
process several times before she starts to get the hang of it.

Important note: many babies *may not get the hang of it* at this age.
No matter how much you try to walk that fine line between putting her down awake and asleep, she may protest at length. If this
happens for more than a few days in a row, just go back to helping
her to sleep, rocking her, feeding her, doing whatever it takes. Her
inability to sleep more independently at this age isn't her fault, and
it isn't yours. Many babies simply aren't able to sleep well

in this "gray area" between being helped all the way to sleep and putting themselves to sleep after going down fully awake. And because we can't expect them to fall asleep completely on their own until after 4 months and 14 pounds, you may have to revert to helping her until she's old enough and weighs enough. Take heart. Although you're probably extremely overtired, you're probably also only a few more weeks away from being able to help her more intensively.

Sleepeasy Solutions for Helping a Newborn Sleep

- There are no bad habits in the first 4 months. Do whatever you need to do to help your baby to sleep.
- For feedings and diaper changes during the night, keep the lights low, and keep your interactions to a minimum. Talking or playing with your baby in the middle of the night will ultimately reinforce her wakings.
- At about 8 weeks, you can begin using a bedtime routine. This is a short, predictable series of events that helps your baby wind down and understand that sleep is coming.
- At about 3 months, you can begin to experiment with putting your baby down drowsy but awake. Soothe her with your voice, or pat or pick her up if she begins to fuss. She may begin to sleep well, or she may not! If she doesn't, don't worry—she'll be able to learn after four months. For now, just help her to sleep however you can.

But I'm Exhausted—How Do I Keep Functioning?

Great question! Believe it or not, the answer is to take care of *yourself* at least as much as you're taking care of your child. Most new parents are much more worried about the baby than about themselves. But remember, you've got a long parenting road ahead of you—and if you don't figure out early on how to refuel frequently, you won't have much left for your baby (or anyone else, for that matter).

"That's great," you may be saying, "but this tiny little creature has non-stop needs, and my spouse is working harder than ever, and there are all these errands and things to do around the house—just how exactly am I supposed to make time for anything else?" Making time for yourself might seem like an impossible task right now. So, here are some ideas:

- Ask a family member to come and stay with you for a while, or ask several to come in shifts.

- Ask a neighbor or good friend to pick up extra items for you at the market or to run a quick errand for you—to the dry cleaner or the post office, for instance.

- Order your groceries online and have them delivered.

- Have a family meeting with your spouse and divide up responsibilities. Can Dad pick up dinner a couple of nights a week on his way home? Can one of you do the dishes while the other one gets the bath started? You'd be surprised at how much more you can accomplish quickly when you divide and conquer the tasks.

- If you can afford a night nurse or a caregiver, spend the money to have someone come into your home. In addition to helping with the baby, many caregivers these days will also do light housekeeping and errands.

- Prioritize what needs doing. Okay, so there's a good inch of dust on your dining room table; the white-glove police are not going to ticket you. Maybe your college girlfriend called you two whole weeks ago; it's fine, you'll call her back eventually. If she's a good friend, she'll understand. (E-mail is a great communication tool during the first few months, too; you can send it at all hours, when you're probably up anyway!)

- If you can muster enough energy to leave the house, consider joining a new-parent group, where you can socialize with other adults and get great information and support. As tired as you may be, you'll likely find that being around people who understand what you're going through feels like a lifeline—and gives you energy to face the rest of your day.

- Take advantage of local resources, such as lactation consultants, parenting centers that offer support groups or educational classes, organizations for parents of multiples, and the like.

- Surf the web, but proceed with caution. There are many wonderful websites for new parents (we list some in "Resources" at the end of this book)—and many of them have chat rooms designed for parents who want to offer one another support—but there are a lot of parents out there who are making decisions that won't jive with your instincts. Take in as much information or advice as you like, but always remember to weigh it against what feels right for you.

The Baby Blues . . . or Something Else?

Taking care of yourself might have an even deeper meaning if you are finding it hard to function at all. This goes way beyond sleep deprivation: you may be feeling teary, anxious, irritable, foggy, or lethargic. You may be overwhelmed by the level of disconnect or conflict between you and your spouse. You may feel unable to care properly for your baby, or that you're having a hard time understanding his needs. All of these symptoms may be signs of postpartum depression, and they are common.

Thankfully, many women—including some celebrities in the last few years—have come forward to talk about their experiences with postpartum depression, which has shed new light on the prevalence of the symptoms. The good news is that it's treatable. It can be hard to reach out for help, especially if you're a woman who's used to feeling competent, capable, and confident. But if you are continuing to find it difficult to make it through the day, it's time to do something. *Now*. Not only is it not good for you to suffer this kind of distress, it's not good for your baby. The first few months are important for forming healthy attachments, and if you're not feeling good, then your baby won't be able to attach to you as closely as he otherwise could. Healthy attachment is a strong predictor of a baby's healthy development. For your sake, and for that of your baby and your family, don't let any more time go by without taking the necessary steps to feel as well as you can. For information on where to find help, please see Resources.

This Is the Hardest It Will Ever Be!

These first 4 months will most likely be the hardest in terms of adjusting to having this new little miracle in your life, figuring out what her needs are and how to meet them, and adjusting to the changes in your family relationships, your work life, your friendships, and the way you identify yourself as a human being. In our new-mother groups in Los Angeles, we constantly remind parents never to underestimate the enormity of the change they've gone through in having a new baby: physically, emotionally, even mentally, you will never be quite the same.

Some of these are welcome changes, of course—you may be finding that you love your baby more than you thought yourself capable of loving another human being—and others may feel overwhelming. For women in particular, who are often the baby's primary caregiver, it can be extremely challenging to have felt organized and capable of making the pieces of your life fit together so nicely before the baby, only to find that no matter how much juggling or rearranging you do, you don't feel like you have any predictability to your day or a handle on just what the baby needs, when. This can really mess with your head, so you've got to fight against letting that happen. These first few months are by far the most chaotic and unpredictable; after 4 months, if she hasn't done so already, and if you wish to, you'll be able to help the baby regulate her feeding *and* sleep, and you'll know her much better—what her cries mean, when she's sleepy, when she'll coo happily in the car, and when she's likely to have a "melt down." So hang in there, and enjoy even the more challenging moments with her as much as you can—they go by awfully fast!

Sleep Month-by-Month

In this section, we're going to give you an overview of developmental information and how it affects your baby's sleep; this knowledge will help you build the foundation you need to help your baby sleep well and will complement the step-by-step sleep instructions in previous chapters. You're welcome to read only about your child's current age range, but if you have the time (and if you're not already so exhausted that all these little words are swimming around like alphabet soup), it's not a bad idea to read the entire chapter, especially if you have a child who's closer to 4 months than to 12. This way, you'll get a nice overview of what the first year looks like in terms of both development and sleep. (To review average sleep needs according to age, please see Appendix D.)

4 to 6 Months

Congratulations! Honestly, we mean it. You've made it through the first several extremely challenging months of having a new baby. When you think about all you've accomplished in the last few months, you really should give yourself a standing ovation. Consider this: you've already changed hundreds of diapers and learned just what position she likes for feeding; you've mastered giving her a bath and begun to understand what she's communicating with her cries; you've shown her off to countless friends and relatives, gracefully answering endless questions about her every gurgle and poop (okay, maybe some of the grace was lost on your mother-in-law, but you can always blame sleep deprivation); and perhaps most heroically, you've tried everything—*everything!*—to get her to sleep well. And even though you've been pushed to your breaking point on several occasions (and probably beyond), you've likely discovered that the love you feel for this tiny creature is more profound than anything you could have imagined.

How Much Sleep?

So just how much sleep does a 4- to 6-month-old need? To develop properly, babies this age should be getting **14 to 16 hours** in a 24-hour period, which breaks down as:

11 to 12 hours of uninterrupted sleep at night (except for a feeding, if your doctor wants you to continue that), and

3 to 4 hours, usually made up in three naps during the day.

That's a lot of sleep! But babies still do a lot of growing during their sleep at this stage, and remember, they need to be getting the right amount of sleep—or what we call good "sleep nutrition"—to be developing to their optimum potential physically, emotionally, and cognitively. At this age, most babies can stay awake about 2 hours in the morning before their first nap, then about 2½ hours between the end of each nap and the start of the next one.

At 4 to 6 months, quality and length of naps take on paramount importance as well. Though your baby may still be capable of napping at the mall or in the car, she now needs to sleep deeply, which isn't possible with ambient noise or motion. (An exception is the third nap, which continues to shorten as she grows; refer back to Chapter 5, "The Art of the Nap.") So, are we saying that you need to be a prisoner in your home, rigidly adhering to your baby's nap schedule? No! You need to balance what your baby needs with what *you* need—and there will be times when you want to meet a girlfriend for lunch during nap time or need to run errands with your spouse on the weekend right when your baby should be going down. It's really fine to have her nap "on the go" once in a while, as long as she's taking good quality naps at home more often than not.

In other words, she's going to need to sleep in the same space each day (unless she goes to day care or another home during the week and is with you for naps only on the weekends) and in a dark, fairly quiet environment. Each of her two to three naps should last at least 1 hour. Why is the length important? One of the main functions of nap sleep is to lower levels of the stress hormone cortisol, which increases with the amount of time a baby is awake during the day. Naps of less than 1 hour are not considered restorative and do not significantly lower levels of cortisol. (For more on cortisol, see page 28 in Chapter 2.)

"Uh-oh . . . My Baby Isn't Even Close to the Totals You've Given"

Don't panic. Together, we'll make sure he starts to get great sleep ASAP, as long as he's 4 months and at least 14 pounds (he needs to meet both of those requirements to do sleep work safely). And here's more good news: he now has the developmental foundation to be able to do some self-soothing—and what's more, because of his brain development, he's now able to remember from day to day what he needs to do to sleep well.

Now, all of that having been said, we do occasionally come across an unusual baby who seems to get by on mostly 30- or 40-minute naps. By "get by," we mean that these babies, miraculously, really do seem rested after a shorter nap and seem alert and awake and happy until the next nap time. One question that we are asked over and over is, "How do I know if my child is getting enough nap sleep?" It's a good idea to use the guidelines for nap sleep outlined in this book, but the definitive answer always lies in the individual child: if she seems rested after the nap and stays awake and alert till the next sleep period, she's doing just fine.

Development

At 4 months, there is good news and bad news. First the good: your baby is now transitioning out of the "fourth trimester" and beginning to wake up to the world around her as she becomes increasingly alert and aware of her surroundings. Her senses are sharpening considerably, and her depth perception is increasing. Her sleep and feeding patterns are beginning to regulate. Her personality is beginning to emerge, and she's becoming more playful with you, delighting in games, and sharing with you the new discoveries she's making each day. It's magical to watch her start to become the person she will be.

Distractibility During Feedings

At 4 months, it may seem as though the baby has lost interest in the breast or bottle. Not true—she's just distracted by sights and sounds that are new to her! The "wow" factor of all the environmental distractions will wear off after a week or two, when she's adjusted to the sensory stimulation. Until then, you might want to try feeding her in a quiet, dark area of your home, or draping a blanket over the two of you in public, to help her focus. You can also allow more frequent grazing, temporarily, until the excitement of her new discoveries starts to calm down.

Now for the bad news. If she's been struggling with sleep up to this point, chances are she will not just outgrow these difficulties with time. Instead, she's going to need your help to sleep well, because her needs are changing considerably.

By 4 months, babies have entered a significant cognitive milestone; their brains are going through an enormous growth spurt, which accounts for all of the increased alertness and distractibility. A baby who used to feed intently will now pop off and on the breast or bottle, turning to look when Daddy or big sister walks into the room or if a noise catches her attention.

At the same time, because your baby is so charged by her new alertness, she may suddenly start waking at night or taking short naps—even if she was previously a great sleeper. Your good old bag of tricks for getting your baby to sleep may suddenly lose their "mojo" altogether. Like many parents, when your baby is 4 to 6 months, you may be doing a lot of praying. If your baby has never slept well, you're hoping that any minute now, she'll just settle into a nice routine; if you have a baby who used to sleep well, you may be trying to convince yourself that all this sleeplessness is just a horrible little phase she's going through.

6 to 9 Months

There are two big areas of change during this age range: (1) developmentally, your baby will begin to grow by leaps and bounds; she'll sit without assistance, comfortably roll both ways, probably start crawling, and begin teething in earnest; and (2) sleepwise, your baby will slowly drop the third nap, making the transition to two naps. We'll talk more about these in just a moment.

When Will My Baby Start Crawling?

The age at which a baby begins to crawl can vary widely. We've met babies who began crawling as early as 5 months and as late as 12 months; both extremes are considered normal, as is everything in between (and some babies skip crawling altogether and simply progress to walking). If you have any concerns about the timing of your baby's motor development, please consult your pediatrician.

How Much Sleep?

At 6 to 9 months, your baby needs **13 to 15¼** hours total in a 24-hour period, which breaks down as:

11 to 12 hours of uninterrupted sleep at night (most babies no
longer need to feed at night at this age), and

2 to 3 ¼ hours made up in two to three naps.

Notice how the nighttime sleep total hasn't changed at all since
the 4 to 6-month age range? It won't actually shift until after 12
months—and even then, not by much. At around 8 to 9 months,
your baby's daytime wake windows will stretch, to 2½ hours between
wake time and first nap and about 3 hours between naps.

Be sure to check with your doctor about nighttime feeds; he or she
may want you to continue feeding at night if there have been any
weight-gain or medical issues, but many babies are ready to wean
nighttime feeds completely at this age.

Motor Milestones and Development

On the surface, you might think that your baby's developmental changes (such as hitting motor milestones like rolling
and crawling) have little to do with sleep. In fact, the two go
together like bread and butter. Each time your baby comes
into a new milestone, it's a double-edged sword. On the one
hand, she's doing a victory dance. "This is amazing!" she
thinks. "I can move my body in this cool new way, and it's all
I wanna do!" Her wake time in the morning may begin to
creep earlier as she enters a lighter sleep phase at the end of
her night and is more easily aroused. "Oh yeah!" she remembers with glee. "I know how to crawl—think I'll practice right
here, right now!" And soon she's up on all fours, revved up
like a thoroughbred before a race. Naps can start to get bumpy
during new milestones as well, as it's hard for her to

slow her body down during the day with all the activity going on.

On the other hand, each time she hits a new milestone it enables her to move her body farther away from you, which is a mixed blessing in her eyes. She's thrilled with her new independence and skills, but she really starts to feel her separateness from you: "Oh my gosh," she thinks, "I'm over here, and Mommy and Daddy are *all the way* over there. I don't like being apart!" If you've ever watched a newly crawling or walking child, what usually happens is they'll take off across the room with reckless abandon, then turn around and check to make sure somebody's still there—or even move back to you for a physical check-in. Then, once she's feeling secure again, off she'll go. It's a mad dance between separation and attachment, and she'll fluctuate back and forth between the two seemingly from moment to moment.

Age-Related Problems and Solutions

PROBLEM: Separation Anxiety

You'll probably notice that you have some mixed feelings about your baby's new independence, too. Not much is written or discussed about a parent's separation anxiety. So just what does it look like? Well, you may find yourself feeling overwhelmed with pride at your baby's new abilities on the one hand . . . and some strong tugs on your heartstrings as you realize that she's starting to grow up and away from you. These feelings are perfectly normal. Talk to other parents—we're sure you'll find that you're not alone in what you're experiencing. But if you start feeling too down, remember that she's still a baby, and still dependent on you in many ways; you haven't been demoted from being Mom or Dad! Separation anxiety, whether for baby or for a parent (usually Mom), is nature's way of preparing us for the inevitable increasing individuation—that's a fancy, clinical term for "feelings of separateness"—in a parent-child relationship. The sooner you can get comfortable with it—and encourage your baby to do the same—the easier it'll be the next time it comes up. You don't want to be the mom who secretly follows the bus as her daughter heads off to first grade!

Tried and true solutions for separation anxiety and sleep disruption

There are a variety of things you can do to help your child manage her anxious feelings about her increasing individuation from you:

- **Play peek-a-boo games.** Play lots of games with your baby during the day that allow her to practice object permanence, or learning that when people or things are out of sight, they still exist. (She won't fully master this concept until age 2.) Engage her in activities that focus on disappearing and reappearing, such as peek-a-boo, jack-in-the-box, or hiding a toy under a blanket and then taking away the blanket so she can see it again. This way, she'll learn that Mommy and Daddy, too, go away but always come back.

- **Always tell your child when you're leaving.** You'll want to communicate all of your separations to your child for the time being. Although it can be tempting to sneak out of the house to avoid a traumatic, tear-filled separation of Scarlett and Rhett proportions, doing so will only make your baby's anxiety worse; at some point he'll look to find you, won't be able to, and won't understand where you've gone, *why* you've gone, or whether you're ever coming back. Instead, be sure to tell him that you're leaving—and if his anxiety is very strong, you'll want to do so even if you're just going to the bathroom or into the kitchen to make dinner. Get right down on his level, make eye contact, and say, "Hi, sweetie. Mommy's going to the bathroom for a few minutes, and I'll be right back!" Let him fuss and squawk for the few minutes that you're gone, then come back and check in again: "Here I am, honey! I missed you, too." It's not a good idea to keep him attached to your hip all throughout the day, even if he seems to prefer that right now, because if he has no chance to practice feeling apart from you during the day, you can bet he'll save it all up for sleep time. (Translation: when you put him down for sleep, he'll make you feel like you're doing a mariachi dance on his tiny, broken heart.)

- **Give your child a lovey.** If you don't already have one, this is an excellent time to introduce a *transitional object* or a lovey (small blanket or stuffed animal) that your child forms an attachment to because it reminds her of you. (For more information on transitional objects, see Chapter 2, "Sleep Stealer #4: Misusing Sleep Aids.")

- **Lengthen your bedtime routine.** Plan to spend a little extra time with him at nap time and bedtime, tacking on an extra 5 to 15 minutes to your normal routine. Give him lots of lap time; hold and cuddle and kiss him so he really feels your closeness. The extra time will also help him wind down his busy body before sleep.

PROBLEM: Teething

Your baby will likely begin teething in earnest during this age range, which can make sleep iffy at best and impossible at worst. Every baby goes through teething differently; some just smile sweetly all the way through, and suddenly one day you notice a tooth has popped through with nary a cloud having darkened her little horizon. Other babies let you know just how miserable they are from the beginning through to the bitter end, crying, whining, drooling buckets, and—worst of all—not doing a whole lot of sleeping.

There are really two kinds of teething: *chronic teething* and *acute teething*. Chronic teething is ongoing; during the first two years of life, your child's teeth are almost always moving through his gums, albeit slowly. During chronic, ongoing teething, you'll notice your child doing lots of drooling, putting just about anything he can fit into his mouth, and gnawing on his fingers or hand. But he will continue to eat and drink normally during chronic teething, and his mood should remain stable (unless he's overtired!). Although your child may experience slight flare-ups in pain or discomfort, this discomfort should *not* be enough to throw his sleep off track.

Acute teething looks markedly different. During acute teething, a tooth is actively cutting through the gum, which is a very painful process for most children. Symptoms can include discoloration, swelling, or translucency in the gums; a clear runny nose or slightly runny diaper; a low-grade fever; pulling on the ear; or a rash around the mouth area (due to increased acidity in the saliva). Children who are acutely cutting a tooth are often less interested in the breast or bottle, or eating solids, as their gums feel sore and irritable when sucking or eating. Your child may also experience dramatic shifts in his mood; he might be playing with a toy happily one minute, then crumble in a torrent of tears for seemingly no reason the next. Your child is experiencing genuine pain in acute teething, so feel free to give him pain reliever if you're comfortable doing so (and after checking with your doctor) and cold or textured objects to chew on. (The frozen-washcloth trick is one of our favorites: wet a washcloth and stick it in the freezer for a few minutes. Kids love the combination of the cold and texture.) During acute teething, your child's sleep—night and day—will likely be bumpy, until the tooth cuts through the gum.

Tried and true solutions for teething and sleep disruption

The good news about teething is that as soon as the tooth has popped through, your little angel's mood will return to normal—and so will her sleep. In the meantime, try the following:

- **Be supportive and available while she's in pain.** During acute teething, your baby will likely have a hard time sleeping through the night or taking good naps. For naps, you can try using motion (swing, car, or stroller) for a couple of days, or holding her while she drifts off, until the tooth cuts through.

- **Use pain relievers.** At nighttime, consider using pain medication (with your doctor's supervision), a topical pain reliever in liquid form, or some nonmedicated teething tablets.

- **Don't work on sleep problems until the tooth appears.** Above all, be sure not to work on sleep or let your baby cry while he's cutting a tooth; he needs your comfort and help at this time, so it's appropriate to give it to him.

PROBLEM: **Starting Solids**

Has anyone said to you, "Oh, just start giving the baby cereal—then he'll sleep through the night!" It's amazing to us how this myth has persisted over decades and generations. Once and for all, *it is not true* that if you feed your child solid food during the day, he will magically start sleeping through the night. If this were true, we wouldn't have needed to start a sleep business! Babies do sometimes wake out of hunger to eat at night, but they also wake for many other reasons that have nothing to do with hunger—and at this age, they should be able to take in all of their milk during the day.

Most pediatricians recommend starting solids at around 6 months, and this may be the point at which your baby starts, too. Adding solids to your baby's diet could affect his sleep—potentially causing night wakings or short naps—only if he has a bad reaction, develops an allergy, or has unusual amounts of gas.

Tried and true solutions for beginning solids and working on sleep

- **Make a plan for solids with your doctor's guidance.** Follow your doctor's advice on how to start and what to start with. Most babies will begin eating rice cereal or oatmeal, then graduate to pureed fruits and veggies. Go slowly, waiting a few days before trying a new food, to gauge any adverse reactions or constipation. We do recommend starting solids during the day (as opposed to dinnertime), so the baby has a chance to "work it out" (poop) during his awake hours and won't be up with a tummy ache at night if he does have a bad reaction.

- **Don't introduce new foods while working on sleep.** When doing sleep learning, hold off on introducing any new foods to your baby until she's successfully sleeping through the night. This way, you won't wonder if she's crying out of pain or discomfort. If you just started giving your baby solids a week ago but are desperate for sleep, stop feeding her solids and come back to it when she's sleeping just fine.

9 to 12 Months

Where's baby? Whoosh—she's scooting across the floor! Zoom—she's dashing from one room to the next! Uh-oh—she's trying to get her fingers behind the fireplace grate . . . again. If only we could bottle a baby's energy at this age and sell it to the rest of us—think of the amazing things we could accomplish!

How Much Sleep?

Here's the picture at 9 to 12 months: Your child will need **13 to 15 hours** total in a 24-hour period, which breaks down as:

11 to 12 hours of uninterrupted sleep at night (if you're still feeding at night at this age, it's probably time to stop!), and

2 to 3 hours made up in one or two naps.

There's still no change in the nighttime total, though her naps may be a bit shorter than they were at 6 to 9 months. At around 12 months, her daytime wake windows will increase, too, to 3 hours between wake time and first nap and about 3½ hours between naps. Almost all babies will have transitioned to two naps by 9 months.

Most don't transition to one nap until after 12 months, so we'll address that change in the next chapter.

Development

Nine to 12 months is all about movement. It's go, go, go from dawn till dusk; at this age, she's crawling, probably pulling to a stand and cruising, and perhaps even walking. It's a big world, and it's your baby's mission at this age to explore every inch of it.

As you might expect, all this activity tends to make most kids think, "Sleep? I've got way better things to do!" Morning wake times and naps may be the first to crumble in times of heightened motor development, due to the baby's excitement about her new skills. Additionally, as your baby continues to be able to move her body more and more efficiently away from you, particularly once she begins crawling or walking (or even thinking about doing so), separation anxiety may reach a fever pitch. You may begin to feel like you have a permanent appendage to your shin, as she clings to you for dear life—when she's not busy ignoring you while she's exploring, that is. And of course, sleep (unless you're cosleeping) is yet another separation, so you may begin to see some serious protesting around going down for a nap or even for bedtime at night.

You might be tempted to assume, if she is resisting her naps, that she's ready to take only one nap a day. Don't even think about it! Not yet, anyway—not till after 12 months,

Safety Proof the Crib

Once your baby starts to pull to a stand, take out your crib bumpers (so he won't use them to help him climb out), and put the mattress on the lowest possible setting. For safety, be sure you've removed all other toys or objects he could stand on.

in most cases. Her resistance has everything to do with the changes going on in her world, not with her body clock's readjustment. And as nature would cruelly have it, because of her tremendous growth spurts, she needs her sleep more than ever.

What to do? You'll want to address both the excitement about her motor skills and the separation anxiety during the day as much as you can. Following are solutions to typical problems for this age.

Age-Related Problems and Solutions

PROBLEM: Hitting a Developmental Milestone

Imagine learning how to fly. You'd be amazed at your new ability—and you'd want to spend every waking moment practicing, exploring, and soaring! Every time your baby hits a new milestone, it feels to him like he's learned how to fly, and it will be awfully hard for him to feel like slowing down.

Tried and true solutions for developmental milestones and sleep disruption

- **Offer lots of floor time.** To help her do her best at sleep time, you'll want to give your baby plenty of floor time to practice, practice, practice all of her new skills during the day. This is *not* the time to have her confined in a stroller or car seat for long periods; she needs to move her body as much as possible while awake, so she won't be as tempted to do so when it's time to sleep. Make sure you've baby proofed your home enough that she can explore without your constant supervision, which quickly becomes exhausting.

• **Give him room to roam.** Let your child have as much space as possible to roam, wander, and discover. Parks, playgrounds, indoor gyms, and other spaces where babies can crawl, climb, slide, and dart around are excellent places to burn off energy.

PROBLEM: Separation Anxiety

Your baby's increasing ability to move away from you makes her acutely aware of the fact that you and she are separate beings. For this reason, whenever she masters a new milestone, you'll likely see a spike in separation anxiety at the same time, which can make her resist going to sleep or wake up during the night wanting to be with you. Unless you are cosleeping, bedtime and naptime also mean separations—so your child may suddenly seem reluctant to part from you when it's time to sleep.

Tried and true solutions for separation anxiety

For a full review on separation issues and solutions for easing anxiety, please see page 142.

CHAPTER EIGHT

Developmental Issues and How They Affect Sleep: Twelve to Twenty-Four Months

W elcome to toddlerhood! Do you remember the day you woke up and realized you no longer had a baby? Instead, you probably found that a curious, often frustrated, incredibly creative small person—clingy one moment, fiercely independent the next—had taken his place. Whether your baby bloomed into a toddler last week or several months ago, or whether your child is closer to 12 months or 24 months, you are now officially the parent of a toddler—and life will never be the same.

We've all heard the horror stories about toddlerhood and the "terrible twos." We've all turned sad, sympathetic gazes toward the mom in the supermarket whose toddler is making noises like someone is hanging him upside down by his toenails because he can't have jelly beans before dinner. But a toddler's frustration and acting out is only one part of the story; you'll also find during toddlerhood that your child is much smarter than you give him credit for (he'll find just the book he wants on the shelf, even if he pulls off the other twenty-five in the process), listens far more than he ever lets on (just wait till he lets rip with a good curse right in front of your neighbor; don't worry, you can always blame your spouse), and is capable of being impossibly, adorably cute as he learns how to dance, talk, and make you laugh.

As for sleep, one of the biggest challenges between 12 and 24 months is getting your child to slow down long enough to get any. Naps can be particularly tricky, usually for one of three reasons: (1) your child is constantly on the go and doesn't want to slow her body down, (2) her separation anxiety spikes up whenever she's doing something new developmentally (like walking or talking), causing her to resist naps, or (3) your child is transitioning from two naps to one and seems neither able to take two naps nor successfully sleep in one longer chunk at midday (for more on this nap transition, see Chapter 5, "The Art of the Nap"). Toddlers this age are also capable of waking up extremely early in the morning, raring to go—and with all of the variables in daytime sleep, your toddler's nights can be challenging as well.

As you devise and implement your Sleep Plan in Chapters 2 and 3, you'll want to consider the developmental issues you'll read about here to help your child's sleep learning progress as smoothly as possible.

How Much Sleep at 12 to 18 Months?

Your child can't stop moving and doing, but ironically, he needs his sleep more than ever. At this age, it's approximately **12½ to 15 hours** in a 24-hour period, which breaks down as:

11 to 12 hours at night, and

1½ to 3 hours during the day, made up in one to two naps.

The best way to tell where your child falls in this range is to watch his energy level, mood, and behavior during the day. If he gets only 10½ hours of sleep at night but seems mainly happy and not cranky throughout the day, you're probably doing fine. If he wakes up after 10½ hours seeming tired or has a hard time making it to nap time, however, he's not getting quite enough night sleep.

You'll notice that a child this age can now stay awake about 3 to 4 hours from wake time till first nap, and about 3 to 4 hours between naps if he's still napping twice a day. If your child has transitioned to one nap a day, he should now stretch 5 to 6 hours from wake up time to nap time. You'll probably need to adjust the bedtime earlier temporarily—by 30 to 60 minutes—as your child adjusts to a longer wake window during the day.

So, a typical schedule for a 13-month-old taking two naps a day might be:

Bedtime: 8:00 PM

Waketime: 7:00 AM

First nap: 10:30 AM to 12:00 PM

Second nap: 3:00 PM to 4:00 PM

A typical schedule for a 16-month-old taking one nap a day might be:

Bedtime: 7:30 PM

Waketime: 6:30 AM

Nap: 11:30 AM to 1:30 PM

Development

At around 12 months, toddlers begin what we call the "Pick Me Up/Put Me Down Syndrome." Here's what it looks like: she's sitting or standing on the floor in front of you, reaching her arms upward with a pitiful look and a plaintive whine that signals, "Pick me up now or I will perish!" So you do, and she's content in your arms for all of, say, 17 seconds. Then she starts wiggling, and squiggling, and whining again, only this time the message is, "Put me down right this second or I will let out a scream so loud it'll make your teeth curl!" So you oblige—but no more than 3 or 4 minutes later, she's back again, wanting up.

So what gives? Welcome to her world: she wants both independence and closeness with you—and neither. She's teeter-tottering back and forth from one extreme to the other as she gets a taste of being a "big kid," then gets anxious about her independence and desperately wants to retreat back into babyland again. Here's a play-by-play from inside her head:

I'm a big girl now—check me out! Here I am walking over to the slide all by myself. I'm not a baby anymore. I don't need help. These steps are kinda steep, but I can do it, and nobody's gonna stop me. Whoa—here I am at the top, and actually it is pretty high up here after all. And wow—Mommy sure looks far away right now. Maybe if I just sit down I'll feel better. But now that I'm sitting down it looks really far to get all the way down to the ground, and you know what? I'm not so sure this is such a hot idea. In fact I think I just wanna get down now. Only I can't go down that huge, long slide all by myself, and I sure as heck am not climbing down those stairs backward. Uh-oh, I have a funny feeling in my tummy. I want Mommy! Waaaaah!

Poor thing. She wants desperately to do things by herself, but she gets easily overwhelmed. She's getting bigger, but the world is still way bigger than she is. This feeling of control and self-mastery followed by lots of self-doubt is extremely confusing for her, and for you it's maddening beyond the limits of even the most patient parent because it often won't be easy to read her mind or understand why she's so overwhelmed or frustrated. Several times a day, you'll find yourself standing in front of an extremely emotional (sad/frustrated/angry/upset/scared) toddler who has no idea why she's feeling the way she is—and you won't quite know what to do about it (sometimes you'll hug her, only to find that she rejects you; other times you'll try to let her work it out, only to find that once you comfort her, she calms immediately).

Aren't you exhausted just from reading this? Well, you're also living it on a daily basis, and on top of the sleep deprivation you're already feeling (we'll get to that in just a moment), suddenly you need exponentially more energy to parent during the day than you ever have before. And you thought being a parent of a baby was hard.

One of the most important things to remember about toddlerhood is that it is a toddler's developmental job to push and test limits. Why? Because he is now moving fully into the process of *individuation*, or separating from you, which he began at about 8 or 9 months (and if you really think about it, it started right at birth). All that limit testing is necessary for him to understand how much power he has (and does not have), and where he ends and where you begin. When he starts pulling handfuls of DVDs off the shelf, and you say no or redirect him, he understands that there's a boundary there. If you decide to just let him pull the DVDs off the shelf (perhaps deciding that there's no danger, so who cares?), he'll find another opportunity to push and test, perhaps by grabbing the cords around the TV and DVD player and trying to pull those. His mantra is, "What can I do? What can I have?"—and he will assume that he can have anything he wants, unless he is told otherwise (by you).

Kids this age are not just being bratty when they test limits. They're learning cause and effect: "If I do this, then Dad does that." If your child drops her sippy cup on the floor during dinner, and you get mad—hey, that's fascinating (to her). Watch her do it again, and again—looking right at you as she does, to see if she can re-create the experience (because it's so interesting). Have you ever thought you might lose your mind because you've already told your toddler for the 18 billionth time not to put her sticky hands on the walls or furniture, and *there she goes again?* It's not just that she wants to push your buttons—though it certainly is mesmerizing to her when you get angry, and your strong reaction (positive or negative) will often serve to reinforce her behavior, whether you realize it or not. She's also probably doing the behavior, in her mind, with some slight variation on the last time she tried: maybe this time it's just her left hand that touches the wall, or this time it's chocolate on her hands instead of banana. If it's different to her, she'll test it out—to see what happens. Cause and effect.

So He's Supposed to Test . . .
What Does This Have to Do with Sleep?

Plenty, actually. First, if your child is pushing and testing throughout the day, he's probably testing at sleep time as well. Nighttime
resistance doesn't usually begin in earnest until after kids start talking more, usually after 18 months—so we'll tackle that in the next
section. What you're more likely to see in this age range is nap resistance, as we mentioned earlier. Second, his enthusiasm about life at
the moment may cause him to wake very early in the morning—
which of course means you're waking early as well. Either one of
these—or both, if you've hit the resistance-to-sleep jackpot can
then contribute to night wakings, due to chronic sleep deprivation.
And if you've been dealing with night wakings since your toddler
was a baby, then you've got one heck of a tangled-spaghetti sleep
situation on your hands.

So let's break this down a bit. Your child is likely resisting naps for
one of three reasons:

1. She's so active and busy during the day that she doesn't want
   to slow her body down for a nap.

2. He's overwhelmed by how fast he's taking those developmental
   leaps forward, and he has some separation anxiety with you.

3. She's transitioning from two naps to one nap, and she either
   doesn't seem tired when she used to or isn't able to stretch out
   her one sleep period long enough to tide her over till bedtime.

Let's take these one at a time.

PROBLEM: Busy, Busy, Busy!

Have you ever noticed how your toddler seems to resemble a race car? He just goes and goes and goes—until he *has* to stop, to refuel (grab a handful of cheese cubes or some crackers) or make a repair (the train he's playing with comes apart, and he needs you to reattach it). But he'll stop *only* long enough to take care of the emergency, then he's right back to the business of busyness.

Napping just doesn't fit into his schedule at this age. "Nap?" he thinks. "How can I nap when I've got to reach the finish line?" The finish line, to him, is to learn and explore as much as he can possibly fit into one packed day—and if he naps, he might miss something *very important*.

Who can argue? Well, *you* can, especially when you see what happens when he doesn't nap (you have probably experimented with skipping naps at least once—and your toddler probably ended his day in a miserable, cranky, tantrum-filled heap). When your child starts to resist naps, it's tempting to assume that he's ready to transition to one nap a day. But it's much more likely that he's just revved up by his new skills—especially if he's doing something brand new developmentally—and he needs a "plan B" till his old patterns eventually return (usually in a week or two). He definitely still needs to nap, so here's how to help with resistance due to not wanting to slow down.

Tried and true solutions for the "Energizer Bunny syndrome" and sleep

Use the following suggestions to help your busy toddler slow down for sleep:

- **Give him the opportunity for *lots* of play time.** Make sure he has plenty of opportunities during the day to use his body and explore. Many children will begin walking during this age range, and when this happens it's like winning the lottery: "Woo hoo!" he thinks. "I've learned how to do this amazing new thing with my body, and it's all I wanna do!" This is not the time to have him confined in a stroller or car seat all day, which will be torture for him. Instead, give him as much space as you can to walk, move, and play. Make sure you've child-proofed your home, so you won't have to redirect him constantly, which can be frustrating for both of you. The more freedom he has between sleep periods, the less likely he'll be to resist the confines of his crib at nap time.

- **Encourage her to practice new cognitive skills during the day.** If the new things she's doing have more to do with cognitive skills (like talking up a storm), make sure to engage her in lots of activities between sleep periods that allow her to practice, practice, practice. Richard Scarry's books are wonderful for this age, as the large illustrations in which every spoon and plate are labeled allows you to sit with your toddler and practice identifying what she sees. Walk through the neighborhood with her, talking together about what you see. If it's puzzles she's into, or building towers with blocks, or lining up all her cars in the "lanes" on your hardwood floor, give her as much time during the day as you can to use her brain and be creative. The more energy she uses up between sleep periods, the better her sleep will go.

- **Offer appropriate choices.** Be sure to give your toddler *lots* of choices right now. He may not be able to tell you exactly what he wants, but he can point. Don't worry—you don't have to let him decide which car you'll buy next, or whether to watch *Sesame Street* or the news. Offer up things that don't matter a bit to you, such as:

- Do you want to wear the green pj's or the blue ones?
- Would you like milk or water in your sippy cup?
- Would you like to put your shoes on first or your coat? (Notice how *not* putting on these things is not an option!)
- Would you like to sit with Mommy in the chair while we read, or on the floor?
- Would you like to skip up to the bath, or walk?

The idea is to give him a sense of mastery throughout his day, so he gets to exercise having an opinion and some preferences. Then, when it's time for you to choose (like time for a nap!), he'll be less likely to resist.

- **Lengthen your wind-down routine.** Add another 5 to 15 minutes to your wind-down routine with him at nap time, and really take your time transitioning him from activity to sleeping. Spend time in his room playing quietly on the floor. Be sure to give him a warning before it's time to go to sleep: "Five more minutes till nap time, sweetie." "Five more minutes till it's time to pick up your toys."

- **Take a break if necessary.** If all else fails and your toddler simply won't nap, try taking a break for a couple of days, and use the car or stroller to allow him to nap with motion. This way, he'll at least get some good sleep in his body, and the change in routine—plus taking a break from slogging it out with you—may be just what he needs to do better in the crib.

PROBLEM: Separation Anxiety

Each time your child can do something new—whether it's moving farther away from you (walking, running), exercising her rapidly growing cognitive skills (talking, learning), or exploring the depths of her expanding library of emotions (feeling very angry or very scared)—it increases her feelings of separateness from you. These new skills signify her new independence, and not needing you as much makes her worry that you won't still be there anyway (just in case she does need you, after all).

By age 2, most toddlers will have fully mastered the concept of *object permanence*, in which they understand that when someone or something goes away, it still exists. But between 12 and 18 months, he's still on his way toward that understanding, and he's not there yet. What this means is that he's still capable of feeling lots of separation anxiety, and it will often spike up just before or during a developmental milestone, then calm down some as the excitement about his new skill wears off a bit. Because sleep is also a separation, his resistance when it's time to sleep may also be tied into his separation anxiety, especially if you've seen signs of clinginess throughout the day.

Tried and true solutions for separation anxiety and sleep

To help lessen his anxiety at sleep time, you'll want to address your child's anxiety between sleep periods as much as possible. In addition to the suggestions found on page 142, try these:

- **Play in your child's room often.** Be sure to play in your child's room during the day, so she won't only associate her room with a place where she's separating from you. Several times a day—not just before or after a sleep period—go into her room and play for 10 to 20 minutes at a time.

- **Give him a picture book.** If your child is very anxious without you, make a small "Mommy Book" that he can look at when you're not around. This can be a small photo album (easy for a child to hold) that contains pictures of you or of you and your child. When you're not there, have Daddy (or your caregiver) look at the book to "check in with Mommy."

Is He Hungry?

If you're concerned that your toddler is waking at night due to hunger from not eating during the day, talk to your pediatrician, or consult a behavioral nutritionist who can work with you and your child to regulate his eating during the day. Even for very picky eaters, though, it's rare that you'll need to feed your child at night at this age.

Settling into Sleep, Night Wakings, and Early Morning Wakings

If your child is having a hard time settling at night or waking through the night, how do you know whether it's separation anxiety or whether your child is just being clever about getting you into the room for a little one-on-one time? Look for cues during the day: if your child is clingy and upset about separating from you when you leave the room, chances are her struggles with nighttime sleep are related to this. (See the section entitled "Problem: Separation Anxiety" in Chapter 7.) If she seems more stable during the day, there's less of a chance that separation anxiety is causing her nighttime disturbances; she may in fact just want a little extra cuddle time with you.

In the latter case, you'll want to make sure you add some extra time to your bedtime routine—perhaps another 10 to 15 minutes—to take your time, hold her on your lap, and let her feel your closeness. If you haven't done so already, try introducing a small blankie or lovey, or a small stuffed animal that she can take into bed with her for comfort. Be careful not to linger too long at bedtime, though, or to hold her each night till she falls asleep.

Another likely culprit of your child's difficulty with settling to sleep, night wakings, and early morning wakings is poor naps. If your child is overtired by the time she goes to bed at night, her body will likely produce the stress hormone cortisol, which can cause her sleep to be choppier and more fragmented throughout the night and can trigger early-morning wakings as well. (For more on cortisol, refer back to "Sleep Stealer #5" in Chapter 2.) Likewise, beware of a very late second nap, which can make it hard for your child to be tired enough to go to sleep at an appropriate bedtime for her age. If she misses the sleep window for her age—the period of time in which she'll settle easily into sleep—her body will begin to produce cortisol. (See chart on page 87 in Chapter 5.) Most children this age need 3½ to 4 hours between the end of the second nap and bedtime.

As for early-morning wakings, some kids do like to rise early, and your busy toddler may be one of them. Due to the "winning the lottery" phenomenon, kids this age wake up raring to go; they can't wait to get started—walking, talking, doing—and get themselves revved up in the crib in anticipation of their busy day. For help in tackling this one, see the section entitled "Motor Milestones and Development" in Chapter 7.

Giving Up the Bottle, Pacifier, or Blankie

For the most part, we recommend weaning to a sippy cup from breast or bottle—or giving up the pacifier or blankie—between 12 months and

17 months, or waiting until after age 3. The time period between 18 months and 3 years old is emotionally tumultuous for children, so it's not a good idea to impose changes during this age range. If your child chooses to self-wean at any age, however, by all means follow his lead. If your toddler is sucking on a bottle or pacifier throughout the day, help him to know that Mommy or Daddy always has arms to hug him when he feels frustrated. A doctor may recommend weaning from the pacifier if a child's speech is not developing properly and he uses it throughout the day.

Whether you choose to help your child wean from bottle or pacifier is an individual decision for each parent. Some are ready to move away from the high maintenance of washing bottles immediately after 12 months, when most children begin drinking cow's milk; others may not mind the extra work and may enjoy the cuddlier aspects of offering a child a bottle. Many parents of toddlers wean to a sippy cup for all but the first and last milk of the day. Allowing your child to use a bottle at these times may help him continue to hang onto enough of the "baby" part of his identity that he feels safer moving toward "big kid" during the day.

Don't work on more than one issue (including sleep) at a time. If you are weaning any of these, be sure not to do sleep learning at the same time. Giving up the bottle, pacifier, or blankie are enormous, significant events for your child, because of the leap forward into a "big kid" mind-set; this is enough for him to tackle at one time. To ensure that the sleep process will go smoothly, wait several weeks after you have weaned either the bottle or pacifier before tackling anything else.

How Much Sleep at 18 to 24 Months?

At 18 to 24 months, children need **12½ to 14 hours** in a 24-hour period, which breaks down as:

11 hours of uninterrupted sleep at night (if you're still feeding at night at this age, it's really time to stop!), and

1½ to 3 hours made up in one nap.

After 18 months, your child may be able to stay awake a bit longer at night, perhaps until 8:00 PM. Don't change the bedtime, though, unless your child is having trouble settling into sleep. If he's still going down at 7:30 and sleeping just fine, then you have the right bedtime! So a typical schedule for a 20-month-old might be:

Bedtime: 8:00 PM
Waketime: 7:00 AM
Nap: 12:30 PM (sleeps till 2:30 PM)

Development

This age begins one of the most turbulent times emotionally that your child will ever go through; it is often referred to as a sort of mini-adolescence. Your child is excited about her increasing independence, and more than ever, she wants to do things her way. At the same time, her limit testing will reach a fever pitch, as she is eager to know which decisions she can now make and which ones are nonnegotiable. The flipside is that this new adventure in her exploration of boundaries can make her feel frightened at times and unsure about being ready to give up being a baby altogether. Just as you did between 12 and 18 months, you may begin to see some separation anxiety develop during this age range both at nap time and at bedtime. This seesaw mind-set can be maddening: one minute she'll want to be picked up; literally the next, she'll want to wriggle away. She wants both closeness and independence, and it's awfully hard to keep up. If your child is showing evidence that she's struggling with separation anxiety during the day, it's likely that her willfulness at night has more to do with fear of separation rather than testing to see if she can get 5 more minutes of snuggle time with you.

If your child isn't exhibiting signs of separation anxiety, limit testing is almost always an issue at this age around bedtime. Toddlers this age may begin to stall bedtime with requests for more stories, more water, or "just one more hug." If your child isn't highly verbal yet, he may simply cry when you try to put him to sleep to see if he can delay your departure, even though he isn't feeling fearful at all.

The good news is that by age 2, most toddlers will have fully mastered the concept of object permanence, in which they understand that when someone or something goes away, it still exists. Understanding this core concept is fundamental to a child's full individuation, after which she has a healthy sense of self and can now meet increasingly more of her own needs (including the ability to emotionally soothe herself in a surprising number of difficult situations).

Age-Related Problems and Solutions

PROBLEM: **Language Burst**

Your child's verbal abilities will likely take off like a rocket during this age range, and suddenly he'll be talking up a storm (most kids have about fifty words by 24 months, though variation is normal; if you have concerns about delay, speak to your pediatrician). This is a good news–bad news situation: the good news is that he'll be able to understand increasingly more of what you're saying (even if he chooses not to listen!); the bad news is that his desire to express himself will still outpace his ability to do so, meaning that his frustration will often build easily and sometimes explode into testing or tantrums.

Tried and true solutions for a language burst and sleep disruption

- **Keep the rules around sleep the same as always.** When it comes to sleep, don't allow your toddler to talk you out of napping or settling down at night with a "No tired!" or "No sleep!" You'll still need to be the timekeeper for both nap times and nighttime. Because his activity level may make his tired cues harder to read, try to watch the clock just as closely as you're watching him, if not more so.

- **Don't interrupt your child's talking in his crib or bed.** Children tend to practice language when they're least distracted, which often occurs in their cribs or beds. Instead of running in to join in the conversation, try to allow your child alone time in which to practice (and enjoy) her new words.

PROBLEM: Separation Anxiety

As your child continues to grow by leaps and bounds, physically, emotionally, and cognitively, she continues to feel confused about the swings back and forth between her growing independence and self-mastery, and her still-ongoing dependence on you. These vacillations can contribute to feelings of separation anxiety, which will spike up intensively at times and seem much calmer at others.

At this age, your toddler is closer to mastering object permanence, meaning she'll understand that when you're not visible in the room to her, you're still somewhere else (in another room, at work, doing errands). But if she's under 2 years, she may not fully comprehend this yet. And because sleep is also a separation, her resistance when it's time to sleep may also be tied into her separation anxiety, especially if you've seen signs of clinginess throughout the day.

Tried and true solutions for separation anxiety and sleep disruption

To help lessen your toddler's anxiety at sleep time, you'll want to address the anxiety between sleep periods as much as possible. In addition to the suggestions on page 142, in Chapter 7, try these tips:

- **Play in her room often.** Be sure to play in your child's room during the day, so she won't only associate her room with a place where she's separating from you. Several times a day—not just before or after a sleep period—go into her room and play for 10 to 20 minutes at a time.

- **Make a special picture book.** If your child is very anxious without you, make a small "Mommy Book" or "Daddy Book" that he can look at when you're not around. This can be a small photo album (easy for a child to hold) that contains pictures of you or of you with your child. When you're not there, have the other parent (or your caregiver) look at the book to check in with you.

PROBLEM: Resistance to Napping or Bedtime

As we reviewed in the section for 12- to 18-month-olds, one major cause of nap or bedtime resistance can be your child's reluctance to slow his body down; he's so busy and wound up from all the activity of his day that he doesn't want to stop long enough to sleep. At this age, another contributing factor can be his preference to be with you over virtually anything else. If he's not experiencing separation anxiety, your child's protests at bedtime are most likely due to some age-appropriate limit testing, as he tries to see how much power he has ("How long can I get her to stay in my room?" he thinks).

Toddlers can go to incredibly dramatic lengths to try to delay bedtime. They may plead inconsolably for more water, another visit to the potty, or yet another story. It can be tempting to give in to what seem like legitimate demands (presented with nails-on-the-chalkboard whining), but delaying bedtime isn't good for him (he needs his sleep) or for you (you need some downtime after a long day, and some time with your spouse).

Tried and true solutions for sleep resistance

Although we elaborate on limit testing in Chapter 2 (see "Sleep Stealer #6"), the following suggestions can also help a great deal:

- **Keep the bedtime routine consistent.** At this age, it's more important than ever to maintain a calm, loving, predictable bedtime routine and consistent boundaries around saying good night. With all of the changes your child is facing during his day, it's very comforting to him to have one thing that he can count on being exactly the same at the end of each and every day.

- **Prepare her before making transitions.** It's a good idea at this age to give your toddler a warning when you're about to make a transition, like going up to the bath or getting ready to go out and do errands. Rather than pluck your child out of one activity and into another, give her a chance to shift gears, so she won't be surprised. Imagine if you were typing an e-mail to a friend and your spouse came along and unplugged the computer. You'd be a tad irritated at best and furious at worst! It's no different for your child: if she's in the middle of "making breakfast" with her pots and pans and you suddenly whisk her away, you'll be much more likely to encounter a "melt down" than if you had given a warning. Simply say, "Okay, honey, fifteen more minutes of playtime, then it's time to go up for nap." "Five more minutes, then we need to put your toys away." It's respectful. It only takes a second. And best of all, it helps your toddler understand what's coming next.

- **Keep stimulation before bedtime to a minimum.** Another cause of your child's resistance may be too much stimulation before bedtime. If your child is used to watching TV or a video just before bedtime, try to move this activity to another time—at least an hour before a sleep period. Believe it or not, even the most calming, lovely video can be stimulating to a child, as it requires multiple senses to process (auditory and visual).

PROBLEM: **Potty Training**

Just as we recommend waiting to transition to a bed until kids are a bit older, the same goes for potty training, too.

To potty train successfully, children need enough verbal ability to be able to tell you when they're wet or dry, and to have words for pee and poop; they also need to be able to stay dry for several hours at a stretch. Most kids don't have these abilities till after age two; the average age for potty training is $2\frac{1}{2}$ years for girls and closer to 3 years for boys.

Tried and true solutions for potty training

• **Don't rush it!** If your child is curious at this age—perhaps she wants to come into the bathroom with you, or flush—encourage her, but don't force her to move forward into actual training until she's showing more signs of readiness, usually after age 2.

• **Use potty words to familiarize your child with the process.** When changing your child's diaper, or when you go to the bathroom, you can use words like pee-pee, poo-poo, dry, wet, or "about to go" to describe what you're doing.

• **Get your child his own potty.** If your child is 18 months or older, purchase a floor potty and tell him that one day, this will be his special potty when he's ready to use it. Put it near your potty, and when you go to the bathroom, bring him with you. He can sit, fully clothed or undressed, on his little potty if he wishes.

• **Read potty books to your child.** There are some excellent children's books that elaborate on the whole potty experience. Reading about other children who use the potty will help most children begin to understand how to use the potty when they're ready. (For ideas, see Resources.)

Developmental Issues and How They Affect Sleep: Two to Five Years

Say *hasta la vista* to babyhood! Sad or exciting as it may feel, your child is probably beginning to look more like a kid than a chubby baby. She's maturing, and no matter how much you may wish she'd stay small, her body and mind are moving full steam ahead. It's easy to see that physically and cognitively, she has been growing by leaps and bounds in the last couple of years. She can do more with her body now, and she can use her language to communicate her needs to the world better than ever. She will continue to test limits (for the rest of your life), and her short- and long-term behavior will be directly impacted by how you handle these difficult moments.

Her physique and smarts aren't the only things that are changing, however. Moving toward preschool age and beyond, it's not quite as easy to spot the *emotional* changes that arise as children develop and embark on different life transitions. Often, children don't (or can't) express what's going on inside of them as they move through change. As you may already know, some of these emotional reactions are endearing, while at other times, you may want to crawl out of your skin from frustration and confusion. In either case, the more armed and prepared you are to understand how growth and change affect your child's emotions and behavior, the better off you'll all be.

Many of the developmental changes and transitions we will discuss in this chapter can affect your child's ability (or willingness) to sleep, so it's important not only to address the behavioral issues but also to understand where she is emotionally during more turbulent times so that you can sensitively attend to her needs. By understanding *why* your child may be having difficulty going to bed or waking at night, you'll make much better decisions about *what to do* in an effective and loving way.

The right amount and right quality of sleep remains *critical* as your child grows. Without good sleep, toddlers, preschoolers, and kindergarteners (and their well-meaning parents) feel lousy. Adequate sleep provides children with the ability to behave better, to pay attention at school and, while playing, to share more easily, and to maintain a better mood throughout the day. On the other hand, when children are not sleeping well, they are usually whinier and crankier, have poor impulse control, and are less adept at socializing. They may get sick more often (due to the effects of chronic sleep deprivation on the immune system) and may be clumsier and more accident prone.

As you create and implement your sleep plan in Chapters 2 and 3, you'll want to take into account all of the developmental issues we describe here. We hope that, armed with this information, you'll be able to clarify why your child isn't sleeping and learn how to most sensitively address any issues that may be impacting his ability to sleep well.

How Much Sleep at 2 to 3 Years?

Sleepwise, your child's needs haven't changed significantly since she was a baby. She still needs approximately **11 to 14 hours** of sleep in a 24-hour period, which breaks down as:

11 hours of uninterrupted sleep at night, and

1½ to 3 hours made up in one nap (if still napping).

Usually between 2 and 3 years, children will start their nap anywhere between 12:00 noon and 2 PM, depending on when they wake in the morning and when their bedtime is scheduled. To be able to deal with their intense and exciting days, they'll continue to need adequate sleep nutrition to cope and to thrive. By the time they near the age of 3, some children will drop their nap altogether, although others may continue to nap for another year or so.

So, a typical schedule for a child this age might be:

Bedtime: 8:00 PM

Waketime: 7:00 AM

Nap: 1:00 PM to 3:00 PM

Development

As your child reaches this age, his development will likely be accompanied by testing and tantrums, and you may find yourself digging deep for patience (see the box that follows).

The Ten Habits of Highly Effective (Little) People

1. If I'm interested in something of yours, it's mine.
2. If I want to go somewhere, I'm going.
3. If you try to stop me, I'm screaming.
4. If you spend lots of time cooking dinner for me, I'll decide I want something else.
5. If my friend wants to share my toys, even if I've *never* shown an interest in them previously, they're mine.
6. If you try to put me in my car seat, I'll scream.
7. If you try to take a toy away from me at the store, I have *every* right to fall on the floor and have a major tantrum.
8. If I see another child eating a cookie, you need to get me one, *now*.
9. If you tell me it's time to sleep, I'll beg you for another hour's worth of activities before I even *think* about going to bed.
10. If I want to come in your bed in the middle of the night, I'll throw every binky and my blankie out of my crib until you cave in.

Sound even *remotely* familiar? We're not sure whether to congratulate you or to empathize with your likely feelings of confusion and being overwhelmed as your child continues to grow and assert himself. This time is filled with tremendous leaps in your child's development, which will be exciting but, at times, very challenging. The changes will include:

- A dramatic increase in expressive language

- Improvement in fine and gross motor skills (he'll be running even faster and may use his increasing fine-motor coordination to program the DVD player)

- Increased curiosity, which translates to an extremely active and impulsive little being (aka "Energizer Bunny Syndrome")

- A newfound desire to make independent decisions (meaning, inevitably, more tantrums)

- Continued enjoyment of parallel play with other children, along with an increasing interest in forming new friendships

- For most, an interest in using the potty

- Beginning preschool (for some), and learning how to separate from Mommy and Daddy

All of these changes will likely feel mind-boggling for both you and your child. The potential downside? Your child's increased sophistication will likely be accompanied by testing, willfulness, and resistance. But how do these behaviors affect sleep?

How Does My Child's Development Affect Sleep?

Along with the daytime battles that children engage in with their parents, bedtime often becomes a struggle as well. While many children have established some good sleep habits up until this point, developmental milestones and transitions can throw off even the most talented sleeper. And if your child isn't experiencing a milestone or a transition but still isn't sleeping well, he's probably just testing limits. In our private practice, we often get frantic calls from parents who claim that their child has become a dictator at bedtime, refusing to go to sleep and requesting more stories, water, and kisses (*or else*).

See, you're not as alone as you thought you were. Many families go through a similar nighttime ordeal. (The kids are lucky they're so cute!)

Less verbal children still in a crib who are simply testing limits may suddenly begin protest crying or resisting at bedtime. The level and intensity of crying can sound as if your child is being tortured, though when picked up she may smile and try to wriggle out of your arms. If this is the case with your child, the problem is behavioral. Follow the instructions in Chapter 3, "Step-by-Step Sleep."

In the age range of 2 to 3 years, it is not only common for parents to have difficulty saying good night without a fuss; it is also common, for those with children who have transitioned into beds, to have little "night visitors" arriving at their bedsides at all hours. For parents who are tired at the end of a long day, this protest behavior is challenging at best and infuriating at worst. As for your child, whose mind and body are growing by leaps and bounds, she needs her sleep nutrition more than ever.

To Transition to a Big Bed . . . or Not

So you just bought some great new sheets and pillowcases on sale in anticipation of transitioning your child to a big bed, and you're thinking that maybe now is the time. You may be surprised to know, however, that we normally do not recommend making this transition until age 3. Unless your child is climbing out of his crib (and you don't want to use a crib tent) or his body needs more space than a crib can provide because he is growing quickly, it's usually better to keep him in the crib, which allows him to feel safely contained. This way, your child can feel confident in his ability to take giant emotional and developmental leaps during the day ("I'm a big kid! Look at me go!") but still regress to the coziness and security of his good old crib at night ("I'm not ready to give up being a baby just yet").

However, if your child has shown lots of interest in sleeping in a bed or has climbed out of his crib frequently, it may be time to make the change. For instructions on how ensure that this transition goes as smoothly as possible, please see "Transitioning a Child from a Crib" in Chapter 10.

How Much Sleep at 3 to 5 Years?

Your child still needs approximately **11 to 14 hours** sleep in a 24-hour period, which breaks down as:

11 hours of uninterrupted sleep at night, and

1½ to 3 hours in one nap, *if* he's still napping.

Some children will push their naps later in the day (say to 2:00 PM), and some drop their naps altogether, although many continue to nap for another year. The best gauge for whether your child still needs a nap is his behavior and mood. If he now seems able to happily make it through the day without becoming either cranky or hyperactive in the afternoon without a nap, he may be ready to make the transition. Another indicator that a child may not need a nap is difficulty in going to bed at his normal bedtime. We've often heard parents complain that they put their preschooler to sleep at 8:00 PM, and he chitchats to himself and his imaginary friends until 10:00. That is often a sign that it's time to give the nap up and move the bedtime even *earlier* (to compensate for the loss of daytime sleep). Once a child has given up his nap altogether, his nighttime need for sleep generally increases by an hour or so.

If your child is still napping, the timing of the nap may depend on whether or not she is in school and what the hours of that school day are. (Some schools offer nap or rest time during the day so that the children can take a much-needed break in between the many activities they participate in.) Many parents we've worked with have enrolled their children in afternoon preschool (from, say, 1:00 to 4:00 PM), which will force them to stop napping if the school offers no rest time. Parents are often concerned about the loss of the nap when starting these programs. We reassure them that their child will get accustomed to *not* napping, but that they need to make sure the rest of her day is calm, peaceful, and not overscheduled—and that they promptly move bedtime ½ hour to 1 hour earlier than usual when the nap is dropped. If your child does not attend school every day, you can allow him to nap at his usual time on the "off" days.

Development

Whew! You made it through the twos. So here's the good news: your child's advanced language skills make it much easier to talk to him and to understand what he is trying to tell you. You can explain that he needs to wait for a moment, or that you'll be back in a little while, and he can actually understand what you're talking about. He can tell you why he is feeling frustrated or sad, which reduces the occurrence of tantrums simply because he can express himself. Parents and teachers can now call upon handy one-liners like "use your words" when a child is acting aggressively or whining. With lots of consistency and repetition (did we mention *lots*?), kids this age usually learn to express their feelings verbally and that "hands are not for hitting." Consequences for behaviors and offering choices become tools you can finally use with some success because you can talk about specific ideas. Your child is starting to develop some self-regulation skills (hooray!), meaning that he can listen to instructions, stop his body from doing the first impulsive thing he feels, and sit quietly for short periods. By the way, these are exactly the skills that will come in handy when you're asking your child to stay in his bed at night.

Now, the bad news. With the onslaught of language and an increase in cognitive abilities, you'd hope that testing behaviors would disappear completely. But rather than disappearing, they've instead taken on a different feel. When a child can talk (and is smart enough to understand just the right way to work you), she can finally ask for things. "One more story," "One more cup of juice," and other such requests can become effective tactics to stall bedtime for even the most steadfast parents. Although children this age typically still want to please their parents, they also want increasing independence and learn that they can manipulate to get what they want. What tenderhearted parent can resist "Just one more kiss and hug, Mommy, 'cause I really, *really* love you"?

Short-Term Perks of Caving In to Demands

So why do intelligent, well-meaning parents give in so easily to their children when demands are made? Well, it's sort of obvious. Saying yes is just plain easier than holding your ground with a no and enduring the screaming and yelling that ensue. When you give in to your child's demands, in the short term, your house may remain quieter and calmer—and let's be honest, it's more fun to see a smile on your child's face than a frown. Moreover, loosening up limits can buy you important shopping time! You may be able to stay at the supermarket longer when you give in to the request for *one more* sparkly cookie. You also don't have to deal with the public humiliation of a screaming child. Sounds pretty good so far, right? Please read on.

Long-Term Repercussions of Caving In to Demands

In the long term, giving a child the ability to make too many choices confuses him and wreaks havoc on your entire family. Letting him be the family "dictator" actually has the opposite effect of what you might think. Having too much power makes him feel frightened and causes him to wonder why the adults in his life can't seem to take control. It teaches him that if he just throws a big enough fit, full of drama and noise, you will cave in simply because you can't cope with intense emotion. He learns that if he feels disappointed or upset, you'll jump to his rescue because those types of difficult feelings are too intolerable for you *or* him to experience. How unfortunate!

Humans are wired to have both positive and challenging experiences and reactions. Everyone needs to learn to cope with all kinds of experiences, including the frustrating or disappointing ones. Preventing your child from feeling frustration or disappointment has grave consequences. If children don't learn how to behave with other people—starting with their parents—they eventually have to learn the hard way, with others who don't care about them and love them the same way you do. They learn through rejection by peers, discipline by teachers and exclusion from groups, all of which affect their self-worth and feelings of competence. If children don't learn to regulate their emotions at home where there is emotional support, they certainly won't know how to deal with them in the real world on their own.

It is now well understood that a permissive household breeds children who are less secure and unable to control their behavior. It takes very conscientious parents to be able to separate their own emotions and reactions from what is best for their children. Unfortunately, our intuition often doesn't tell us that allowing our children to learn to accept limits gives them the opportunity to learn one of life's most important lessons. Yet understanding limits helps children learn to be confident and successful.

Separating Your Feelings from Hers

For parents who have had a lot of disappointment or neglect in their own childhoods, setting limits with their children can feel especially difficult. It can be hard to distinguish what is appropriate limit setting from neglect or abandonment. As you work on helping your child to sleep, you will need to set limits and stay consistent. If you suspect that your own challenging feelings may surface as you set limits with your child, you might want to consider talking with a parent educator or counselor who can help you distinguish between your own negative experience versus what is healthy and appropriate for your child. Doing so will help you help your child succeed in learning how to sleep.

The Healthy Side of Limit Setting

When you need to hold your ground with your child, try to frame the experience in a positive light. Difficult times often offer wonderful opportunities for "teachable moments." What is a teachable moment? It is a time when your child is struggling with something that feels difficult but, with your guidance, moves through her experience to gain a skill or learn a necessary life lesson. As much as you believe that helping your child to get her needs met and to feel loved is important, it is also important to understand that her frustration can lead to greater self-esteem as she finds her motivation to learn something new. With sleep, once you've explained the rules around bedtime and given your child a nice bedtime routine, she'll feel some frustration as she learns that Mommy and Daddy will hold to the rules and that she can cope with those limits. The upside is that she'll then also be able to learn how to become a great sleeper.

Transitions for Toddlers and Preschoolers That Can Affect Sleep

Major transitions at this age that affect sleep include the arrival of a new sibling, beginning potty training, starting preschool, and transitioning to a bed. Unresolved feelings about all of these issues can lead to separation anxiety and can cause fears at bedtime, protesting behavior, and night wakings.

Whenever possible, avoid allowing your child to take on more than one of these big changes at a time. For instance, if your child is beginning preschool, don't simultaneously transition him to a bed or take away his pacifier; wait at least a month to instigate the next big change.

Creating Books to Help Ease Transitions

Making a book with your child (or purchasing a made book on the topic in question) is one of our favorite tools to help your child process her feelings about whatever change is happening. (Don't worry, it only takes 5 minutes—and no, you don't have to be an artist!) The book also allows you to empathize with her feelings. It doesn't have to be fancy; you can draw stick figures, use photos, whatever you like—have fun with it! Simply tell the story of the change that is happening in your child's life and how hard it can feel for her, and include some possible suggestions on things she can do or ask for to feel better. Putting the experience into words will help her not only feel better but also sleep better, too.

Here's an example of a book for Jake, a child transitioning to kindergarten (and having trouble sleeping due to anxiety).

"In a couple of days,
Jake will start Kindergarten!"

"Jake's teacher is named Miss Susan.
She is very nice and helpful to children."

"Jake's friends, Rebecca and Ryan, will also be in his new class. They were in the same class with Jake at preschool."

"On the first day, Jake and Mommy will go to school together. Mommy will take Jake to his classroom and stay for a few minutes, until Jake feels comfortable with his teacher and his new friends."

"Mommy remembers when she started her first day of kindergarten! She had a funny feeling in her tummy, and she wasn't so sure she'd like it. Lots of kids feel just the same way. It ended up being really fun. She read books and played on the playground. Mommy couldn't wait to go back the next day."

"At school, Jake and his class will have circle time, play outside, and sing songs."

"When the day is done, Mommy will pick Jake up, and he can tell her the fun things he did at school."

Important to consider: Try not to read this kind of book *too* far in advance of a big change, as doing so can cause increased anxiety. Beginning the day before the change begins is best.

You can also find books on a variety of children's issues at your local bookstore. Look for books on such topics as friendships, divorce, death and dying, moving, and having a new baby, if your child is dealing with any of these issues. (See Resources for recommendations.)

Age-Related Problems and Solutions

PROBLEM: Fears

Between the ages of 2½ and 5, children become very imaginative. You may notice that your child engages in fantasy play, acting out detailed scenarios with his toys. This type of play helps children to deal with emotions and to feel a sense of control.

Increased imagination can also cause all kinds of fears to arise. It can be difficult for a child to separate what is real from what is fantasy, and sometimes children begin to have trouble falling asleep or to wake at night. Sometimes a child's fears are based on reality. If a grandparent passes away, for example, a child may become afraid that Mommy or Daddy may die and have a hard time separating at bedtime. Other typical fears include fears of the dark, monsters, sharks, scary dogs, and spiders. Because bedtime is when children separate from you and (usually) sleep alone, it is a common time for anxieties to manifest.

It can feel overwhelming for parents wondering what to do. On the one hand, you certainly want to support your child when he is afraid, but on the other hand, you don't want to reinforce his belief that there is actually any danger. It's important to be patient and to allow your child to express his feelings; they may not be logical to you, but they make perfect sense to him, and if you push them away he will only become more anxious. If you take your child's feelings seriously by listening and then reassuring him that he is safe, your child's anxieties—and sleep problems—will typically pass fairly quickly. Once you've noticed that your child's fears are decreasing, ease up on your attention to them, to avoid reinforcing prolonged bedtime rituals or middle-of-the-night wakings.

Tried and true solutions for fears at bedtime

- **Help desensitize your child to her room at night.** If your child's fears are intense, you can sleep in her room for a few nights. Set up a bed for yourself on the floor by her crib or bed. If your child is in a bed, avoid sleeping with her, as doing so will prevent her from gaining confidence—and overcoming her anxiety—by sleeping alone. When you both wake in the morning, explain, "See—your room is safe. Nothing happened, and everything is just fine. Your room is a really cozy place to be!"

- **Play in your child's room during the day.** Be sure to play in your child's room during the day so it is not only a place where he must separate from you at night. With frequent play sessions in his room, he'll feel safer and more comfortable being in his room during sleep.

- **Let there be light.** If darkness feels frightening for your child, install a night-light or leave an overhead light on a dimmer, or keep the door ajar to a dimly lit hallway to help her feel more comfortable.

- **Play with shadows.** To demystify nighttime and darkness, play with your child in the dark with a flashlight, perhaps doing finger puppets in the shadows or singing songs with the dancing light.

- **No more scary stuff!** Avoid anything remotely scary, including videos, television, or books, during the day.

- **Talk about it.** If your child is verbal enough to discuss what he's frightened about, talk with him during the day about his fears. Be careful not to suggest something that he might be afraid of without his mentioning it first. He may hook into your idea and either become afraid of whatever you've mentioned or begin to use it as a reason not to go to bed.

- **Ditch the "monster spray."** If fears are related to monsters, assure your child that *monsters are not real—they are just pretend.* You can even paint his face green (with some face paint), and tell him, "See, you can even pretend you're a monster by putting green paint on your face!" We do not advocate "monster spray," which only confirms for the child that there may in fact be real monsters.

- **Give your child a lovey or transitional object to hold and cuddle.** It can be extremely comforting for children to cuddle a stuffed animal or favorite blankie when they're feeling fearful at night. These transitional objects serve as a bridge between parents and children while they're separate and allow a child to self-comfort at times when she needs a little extra support.

- **Make a book.** Write a story about the feared subject to further reassure your child about whatever frightens him. (See the previous section entitled "Creating Books to Help Ease Transitions.")

PROBLEM: Nightmares

If your child has a nightmare in the middle of the night, he will wake up and need your comfort. All children have nightmares at some point as their imaginations develop. Nightmares often occur during some major event in the child's life, like starting school or a parent's departure for a work-related trip. When your child has a nightmare, he will need your comfort, hugs, and reassurance.

Tried and true solutions to decrease nightmares

- **Try to keep stress to a minimum.** When a child goes to sleep with a great deal of stress, he may manifest these anxieties in the form of nightmares. Try to help him process whatever may be making him anxious during the day. If the nightmares continue, consult a counselor who may be able to help him process his feelings.

- **Avoid scary stuff.** If your child is waking at night frightened, take a break on scary books, videos, and TV. Even the evening news can trigger anxiety for your child.

- **Leave the lights on and the door open.** Although you cannot avoid nightmares completely, it may be reassuring for your child when she has a nightmare that the room is not too dark and that she feels she has access to you should she need it.

- **Make a dream catcher.** If nightmares have become a frequent occurrence, help your child to make a dream catcher or some other object that helps to "ward off bad dreams" and help him feel more protected.

- **Make sure your child is getting enough sleep.** Lack of sleep can increase nightmares. If your child has a late bedtime, try moving it earlier. If your child has recently given up naps, try to give her a short snooze in the car to help her make it to bedtime.

- **Offer reassurance.** If your child does have a nightmare, go to him and cuddle him. Remind him that you are right nearby in your room and that he's safe. Reassure him that the dream was not real. Help him to calm down and feel comfortable before leaving the room.

PROBLEM: **Night Terrors**

Night terrors occur in a small percentage of children. They are not nightmares and need to be treated differently. Lasting usually no more than 15 minutes, terrors are often inherited from a parent who had them in his own childhood. Although night terrors are extremely upsetting for parents to witness, your child is not in any real danger. These episodes are not psychologically based, and children have no memory of night terrors once they've awoken. Night terrors usually occur in the first several hours of your child's sleep; she may appear to wake with a sudden jolt, but because she is not actually awake, she may cry, scream, or thrash her body but will be unable to answer you or hear you. Usually, night terrors decrease as children get older. The following are factors that may contribute to night terrors:

- Sleep deprivation

- Irregular bedtime and wake time

- High fever or other illness

- High levels of stress during the day

Tried and true solutions for handling a night terror

- **Stay near your child, but don't wake him.** Stay close in case you need to protect your child from harming himself while he is thrashing. Waking him, however, is dangerous because doing so will only cause him to become frightened. If your child sleepwalks during a night terror, you may want to secure the door of his bedroom with a safety gate to keep him from walking around the house and potentially hurting himself.

- **Try to reduce stress in your child's life.** If your child is involved in an overabundance of activities and seems stressed by busy days, you may want to cut out a few play dates or shorten her days at preschool for a while. If there are bigger issues at home, such as divorce or a move, try to process these events with your child so that she can work through some of the stressors with you.

- **Watch for overfatigue.** Try to keep your child's bedtime early to avoid the effects of cortisol (see page 28 for more on cortisol). Spend some extra time with him in the morning once you've all had a good night's rest.

PROBLEM: Separation Anxiety

Whether you have a 2-year-old or a child closer to 5, your child may be experiencing separation anxiety because he's taking giant leaps forward in his development or handling a major transition. If your child seems needy or clingy, he may need to touch base often and refuel his connection to you, much like a car stops at a gas station to refuel and then keeps moving on. For some children, just seeing Mommy across the room is enough to feel secure, while others need some direct physical contact. Once your child feels confident again, he will venture off and continue normal exploration.

Tried and true solutions for decreasing separation anxiety

- **Encourage the use of transitional objects.** Blankies, teddy bears, or other beloved objects can serve as a much-needed bridge between parent and child while they're separated during the day *and especially at night*. If your child has not attached to a particular object, you can encourage him to sleep with one of his favorite stuffed animals or buy him a special "Mommy Bear" that he can hold and hug whenever you are apart, including bedtime. (For more on "Mommy Bears," see page 36.)

- **Make a kiddie photo album.** Make a small album for your child with pictures of her with Mommy and Daddy. Tell your child she can look at the pictures of you when you're not home, or look at the book together before bedtime.

- **Don't sneak out!** To prevent bedtime struggles and protect nighttime sleep while your child is experiencing separation anxiety, always tell your child when you're going away and when you come back. With repeated practice at separating, he will learn that Mommy and Daddy go away, but they *always* come back.

- **Spend extra cuddle time before bed.** Lengthen your bedtime routine (by about 10 minutes) to allow your child to have a little bit more time with you before separating for the evening.

- **Don't start sleep learning if anxiety is high.** If your child is experiencing intensive separation anxiety during the day, this is not a good time to begin sleep learning. Wait until her anxiety begins to calm down during the day.

PROBLEM: Anxiety About Starting School

Somewhere between 3 and 5 years of age, many children begin to attend preschool; children closer to 5 may begin kindergarten. These new experiences offer opportunities for enrichment, friendship, and competence. One major learning opportunity in going to school comes with beginning to feel comfortable separating from Mommy and Daddy. For children who have not attended any type of day care prior to preschool, separation from parents can be truly anxiety provoking (and even harder for the parents!). Even for a 4- or 5-year-old who has attended school the previous year, or a child who has been in a day care setting since he was a baby, the beginning of a new school year can often cause anxiety. Attending elementary school is a giant leap for preschoolers who may have felt comfortable and familiar with a smaller, more nurturing environment and fewer academic demands.

When children begin this monumental transition, their anxiety can cause a temporary disruption in sleep. When your child is acclimating to a new school, don't begin to iron out sleep difficulties simultaneously. Give your child a couple of weeks to get comfortable at school during the day before you also ask him to maintain more emotional control at night. Once he seems happy and relatively well adjusted to his new school, you can then begin to work on sleep in earnest.

Tried and true solutions for easing the transition to school

- **Help your child get to know the class.** If possible, visit your child's school prior to the beginning of the school year to meet the teacher, or schedule some play dates with other children who will be attending.

- **Find out how separation is handled at your child's school.** Ask about the school's policy on separation. Our preference, especially when a child first begins preschool, is for the parent to stay as needed until the child builds her relationships with teachers and confidence in herself to play and learn in her new environment. Once she's more comfortable, parents can leave for brief periods of time, and they can work up to a full day once their child has had some success with short separations.

- **Make a book.** The start of school is an excellent time to make your child a book (as mentioned previously in this chapter). You can include pictures of his new teacher, the front of the school, or the new friends that he will get to know. Write a short story about starting school and how you will help him. Mention that you will pick him up at the end of each day. As discussed previously, there are also a number of published books for children that address the beginning of a new school year.

PROBLEM: The Birth of a New Sibling

The birth of an additional child is a joyful and wonderful time for families but can also bring up many difficult feelings for the older child. Children who have been accustomed to receiving most of the attention and who have not needed to be very patient in the past now have to learn some serious (and wonderful) life lessons. We frequently hear from second-time parents that they feel guilty about imposing an additional member of the family on their toddler or preschooler and that they fear the "dethroning process" will destroy their older child's spirit.

But this is one of those teachable moments. The arrival of this new baby can provide wonderful opportunities for your older child to move through a transition and for you to empathize with your child's feelings, allow him to experience some frustration and sadness, and learn that he can accept and cope with the changes.

Out of guilt, parents often begin to allow boundaries to unravel when it comes to bedtime and where their child sleeps. Guilty as they may feel, however, parents need to maintain consistent rules and structure to allow their toddler or preschooler to feel safe and secure. It is tempting to allow an older child into your bed at night, though if you're wanting to stay closer to your child temporarily, it's best to sleep in his room.

Tried and true solutions for easing the arrival of a sibling

- **Prepare your child for the upcoming event.** Prior to the arrival of your new baby, purchase a book on siblings. You can also make a personalized book that explains that the baby is coming, who will stay with your child when Mommy and Daddy go to the hospital, and what life might look like when you get home (see "Creating Books to Help Ease Transitions," earlier in this chapter).

- **Bend sleep rules, but don't break them.** During the first month or so after the baby is born, one parent may need to sleep in the older child's room or visit frequently during the night if she is having a strong reaction or is especially clingy. However, even though you may have to "bend the rules" with additional visits or sleepovers for a while, try to maintain as much of your normal routines as you can. Keep the timing and location of sleep the same as always. If your child is upset by her sibling sleeping in your room, tell her that when she was a baby, she needed to sleep close to Mommy, too, so she could drink lots of milk at night. Assure your older child that when the baby is a little bit bigger, he will move to his own room, just like she did when she was ready.

- **Get back on track when it's calm.** Once some semblance of normalcy returns to the household, help your child to remember that you're in charge at bedtime. Because rules help children feel safe, it is important to remind your older child that he goes to sleep at night in his bed by himself and wakes up when the sun is bright in the morning.

- **Keep children under age 3 in the crib.** Remember, we recommend keeping your older child in her crib until she is closer to 3 years old, even if you need to get an additional crib or create another temporary sleep environment (like a playpen or cosleeper) for the new baby. The crib represents a cozy, babylike environment for your older child, who is being forced to grow up quickly in many other ways. This is not the time to pull an additional comfort item away from her; she needs time to adjust to the new baby.

- **Highlight the benefits of being older.** Try to point out, when possible, that the baby can't do many things that your older child can do. Explain that babies can't go out for an ice-cream cone, babies can't go down the slide, and babies can't play with the family dog.

PROBLEM: Potty Training

Potty training is another example of a major transition that would preclude working on sleep at the same time. Give your child a couple of weeks to feel more in control of his body during the day before you also ask him to maintain more emotional control at night.

Although the average age for completing daytime potty training ranges from 28 to 36 months, nighttime training very often comes much later—even years later! Kids' brains have an easier time recognizing when their bladder needs to empty itself during the day than they do at night. Most pediatricians indicate that it is normal for a child not to complete nighttime potty training until 5 or 6 years old. Feel free to use a diaper or pull-up at night until your child can remain dry throughout.

Tried and true solutions for helping your child sleep once he is potty trained

- **Limit liquids before bedtime.** Tell your child that he needs to stop drinking after dinnertime. A small sip of water with brushing teeth is okay, but make sure not to allow him to take in so much liquid that he'll be up throughout the night.

- **Visit the potty right before bed.** Once you've completed your bedtime routine and before you give your child final kisses, tell her to try to use the potty one last time before bed. If she has trouble, you may want to try to turn on the water faucet in the bathroom, as hearing the sound of water will typically encourage a child to urinate.

- **Watch for limit testing.** If your child claims he has to go to the bathroom once you've left the room, take him once, but then tell him he's all done until the morning. Some children find that claiming they need to go to the potty will extend bedtime and will come to rely on this excuse.

- **Rehearse going to the potty.** Do a rehearsal during the day of the plan for going to the bathroom during the nighttime hours. Show her how she can go to the bathroom at night and return to bed on her own. You may want to leave a night-light on for your child or a hall light so she can see where she needs to go to relieve herself and then go back to bed without needing to wake you. Make sure that your child is *completely comfortable* using the bathroom before you ask her to try it by herself.

Thinking About Transitions and Sleep

If sleep problems have cropped up because of one of the transitions we've mentioned or because of extreme separation anxiety or fears, wait until things calm down a bit before working on sleep. If your child is unusually anxious about a change (sleeping in a new, unfamiliar room, or beginning school, for example) or is experiencing a fear of monsters or the dark, you can offer extra support by sleeping in his room on a mattress on the floor *temporarily* (until you notice the anxiety decreasing during the day), or check on him during the night as needed. Avoid sleeping in his bed with him or allowing him to sleep in your room, as doing so can make the return to independent sleeping in his own bed difficult.

CHAPTER TEN

Special Situations

This chapter is designed for those of you who need a bit of extra information to ensure sleep success. Whether you're a parent of multiple children (born at the same or different times), a single parent, or dealing with a baby who has reflux, you'll find answers here to questions about how to adjust or modify how to respond to your child (and take care of yourself).

The second section of this chapter, entitled "Bumps in the Road," covers the inevitable, unexpected wrinkles that, if not addressed, can thwart your progress. Whether these bumps occur in the middle of sleep learning or later, the information covered here should have you back on track in no time.

Colic and Reflux

The truth about colic is that medical professionals don't really know what it is or what causes it. It's a kind of catchall term that is used to describe a baby who cries more than most babies do in the first few months of life. Colic can make the exhausting job of being a new parent even more exhausting, as it's heartbreaking and maddening to feel that there's nothing you can do to help your baby calm (let alone sleep). We highly recommend Harvey Karp's *The Happiest Baby on the Block* book and DVD to help with these issues. You won't be doing intensive sleep learning with your baby until after 4 months, and the good news is that most babies will have outgrown colic by this age anyway. After 4 months, it's perfectly fine to use the methods outlined in this book to help your child sleep, even if he's been colicky as a newborn—though we have noticed that *some* (not all) colicky babies cry a little longer and a little harder than others. We say "a little" because the increase is not significant, and if you are consistent with your sleep plan, your child should still learn how to sleep in a few nights (remember, naps always take a bit longer). If you'd like extra reassurance, speak to your pediatrician before starting.

Reflux is very common, especially in young babies. Babies 4 months and older may be given a diagnosis of reflux if they spit up more often than not after a feeding, if there are signs of discomfort during or after a feeding (such as excessive crying, refusing the breast or bottle, or arching their back or stiffening their body), or if they are able to take only small amounts of milk at a time. (There are other symptoms, as well; talk to your pediatrician if you are concerned that your baby may have reflux.) If your baby does receive a diagnosis, your doctor may prescribe a medication to help manage her symptoms; most babies with reflux respond well to medication, and symptoms then fade. Alternatively, you may be able to manage your baby's symptoms by altering your diet (for breast-feeding moms) or finding a formula to which she responds well.

If your baby does have reflux, be sure to talk with your doctor before using the methods outlined in this book—though except in extreme cases, it should be perfectly safe to do so as long as your baby is being treated appropriately for the condition and isn't experiencing pain. Your doctor will likely advise you to hold the baby upright for 10 to 20 minutes after a feeding, in which case you'd want to budget enough time in your bedtime routine to include this extra time and still be able to put your baby down at the appropriate bedtime. If you are weaning feeds in the middle of the night, you don't have to keep your baby awake as you hold her upright. Just return her to her crib (or bed with you) when the appropriate amount of time has passed.

Your doctor may also suggest elevating your baby's crib or using a wedge that goes under the mattress. Similar to holding your baby up after a feeding, these options use gravity to help your baby's digestive system function as efficiently as possible.

The vast majority of babies outgrow reflux eventually, usually at around 6 months. But with your doctor's approval, you should be able to use this book to get plenty of good sleep before then!

Vomiting

Some children (usually babies) get so worked up in protest crying that they vomit. For both you and your child, this can feel like adding insult to injury; the crying is hard enough all by itself, and on top of that your child now seems to be in serious distress, which is very upsetting for all of you. The good news is that if your child hasn't previously been prone to vomiting when crying, chances are that she won't suddenly start doing so now. So thankfully, you probably won't have to face this situation.

If it does happen, however, by all means go in to clean her up and change her pj's, but try not to rush in hysterically the moment your child vomits. (Remember, she's not sick; she's just having a physiological reaction to the changes she's experiencing.) As painful as this might be for you, by waiting a moment or two, you avoid reinforcing the behavior so that your child doesn't begin to think vomiting is the way to get you to change your tune. Remove the crib sheet and replace it with a fresh one. But don't linger too long, and just calmly say, "Oh, honey, you threw up. Mommy will change you." Then put her back in her crib, leave the room, and resume with your check-ins.

Yes, you heard us right! Although she's clearly upset (because she's protesting change and because she hasn't yet learned what she needs to do to soothe herself to sleep), her vomiting does not mean she's not ready or able to learn. It simply means that she's a particularly sensitive little being, and she's feeling her frustration a little more intensely than another child might. She's really okay, and continuing to work on sleep immediately following a vomiting incident is just fine. (Of course, if you have any reason to suspect illness—perhaps you saw a telltale symptom or two during the day, for instance—stop sleep learning and call your pediatrician.)

Over the years we've often been asked whether a child can vomit on demand repeatedly, as a way to manipulate parents back into the room. Although this is possible for some clever children, the more likely scenario, especially after 9 months, is that the behavior is inadvertently being reinforced. If Mom and Dad fuss and swoon when their child vomits, and hold her at length till she calms again, she quickly learns that vomiting will earn her some extra attention.

Pooping

Here's a familiar scenario we've encountered often: the baby is finally beginning to go down smoothly for his naps, crying little if at all, sleeps for a solid 40 or 45 minutes, then wakes crying, having pooped. If we had a dollar for every time pooping had ruined a nap or caused an early morning waking, we'd be inventing a "poop sensor" just for this purpose!

You can't control your child's bodily functions, but you can maximize his ability to go back to sleep by handling the situation swiftly. If you've determined that your child has pooped (usually you can smell it during a check-in), get him up, change him quickly *without talking or interacting*, then put him back down again. If he's had most of a nap or close to a full night's sleep, the probability that he'll go back to sleep is low. However, what you are teaching him is that no matter what, *you* determine wake-up time.

If there is more than half an hour left before that sleep period is over, be patient. Do your check-ins if you'd like (though some parents find that extending the intervals of check-ins following a poop incident works best, as changing him is quite stimulating), or just leave him be. Eventually, he should learn to go back to sleep.

That having been said, there are some kids who are what we call "punctual poopers." They poop on time, every day, at exactly the same time. If you are unlucky, this time might be 5:30 AM (and your target wake time might be 6:00 AM). If you are feeding your child solids, watch what he's eating right before bed; fruit or high-fiber foods might be contributing to the early-morning poop. If your child *never* goes back to sleep, even after a week or ten days of consistent response from you, you might need to settle for the early wake time, in which case you'll want to adjust the bedtime a bit earlier to make sure he's at least well rested at that hour. In desperation, some of our parents over the years have experimented with allowing their child to sit in a soiled diaper if the pooping occurs very close to the scheduled wake time (say, within an hour). If you feel comfortable trying this, you can—though you'll want to keep a close eye on any developing diaper rash. Unfortunately, we haven't heard of many kids being able to sleep in a soiled diaper.

Transitioning Your Child from Your Bed to Hers

If your child has spent much more time in bed with you than in her own sleeping environment, or has *never* slept in her own room, follow these guidelines:

- Spend a week playing in your child's room during the day. Make this room the central play place in your home, temporarily. You want this room to feel comfortable and safe to her, and you *don't* want her to think of it as only a place where she separates from you. Put your child in her crib with toys from time to time, but stay very close. If she can tolerate only a few minutes at first, don't force it; take her out and try again later. Try to gradually increase the time in which she can feel comfortable in her crib. If your child sleeps in a bed, spend time playing or reading on the bed.

- When you are noticing that your child is enjoying herself consistently playing in her room, and in her bed or crib, one parent should plan to spend two to four nights sleeping in the room with your child, *continuing to help her to sleep the way you always have.* In other words, all that changes during this step is that you are sleeping in her room; you can still feed her to sleep, rock, bounce, and so forth. Whenever your

child wakes throughout the night, help her back to sleep the
way you always do.

- After several nights of helping your child this way, it is time to
begin your sleep plan. Proceed according to the guidelines in
Chapter 3, "Step-by-Step Sleep."

Transitioning Your Child from a Crib to a Bed

Although it may be tempting to begin thinking about transitioning your active toddler to a "big bed," we do not recommend doing so
until age 3. Unless your child is climbing out of his crib or needs more
space than a crib can provide because his body is growing quickly, it's
better to keep him in the crib, which allows him to feel safely contained and babylike. This way, your child can feel comfortable taking
giant developmental leaps forward during the day but still regress to
the coziness and security of his good old crib at night. Also, until age
3, toddlers are extremely impulsive, and your child's difficulty in
understanding and being able to follow directions or rules (like staying in bed all night) will make sleeping in a bed challenging at best.
If you transition to a bed before age 3, you can pretty much plan on
waking up to a little visitor next to your bed each night.

If your child is climbing out of the crib, however, you have a safety
issue. You can either use a crib tent, which fits onto the top of the crib and
safely contains your child in the crib, or make the transition to a bed early.

Before putting your child into a bed, make sure that there aren't
any other big changes going on in his life simultaneously. For
instance, if your child is in the middle of potty training, you have a
new baby coming (within two months), preschool is about to begin,
or you've just moved or are about to, these are not good times to

make the change. Please read Chapter 9 for specific information about these milestones in your child's life.

To help your child transition smoothly to sleeping in a bed, follow these steps:

- **Step 1: Safety proof.** Adequately safety proof your child's room and any adjacent areas he may be able to wander into in the middle of the night. You'll want to secure tops of stairs, windows that are normally ajar, or stepstools that can be tripped over. If you feel concerned that your child will be unsafe if he wanders, install a safety gate at your child's door to prevent this. (For more on safety gates, please see page 36 in Chapter 2.) You can install a small night-light in your child's room to help him orient himself to his new bed should he wake in the night, and to avoid any bumps or bruises if he should decide to get up and walk around his room.

- **Step 2: A mattress shopping we will go.** Go to the mattress store, and have your child help you pick out the mattress or bed. Although many families like the "wow" factor of a racing car or princess bed, it's not necessary to buy a frame at this point; all you need is a twin-size mattress and box spring and some safety rails for the side. This new bed should sit low on the floor for quite some time as your child adjusts to being in her own bed and so there won't be a risk of her falling off; she'll also be able to get in and out of bed more easily. Get some fun new sheets, or a special pillowcase. Avoid labeling this new bed a "big boy" or "big girl" bed, as this language can frighten a child who already feels anxious about taking leaps forward in her development. Refer to it instead as simply "your new bed."

- **Step 3: Buy a bed buddy.** Allow your child to pick out a special "Mommy Bear" or "Daddy Bear" to sleep with in the new bed. This may feel like an acceptable alternative to *you* getting in bed to sleep with him. When you put your child to sleep, remind him that "Mommy Bear" is going to cuddle with him all night, and when he wakes up, Mommy or Daddy will come to check on him.

- **Step 4: Dismantle the crib (together!).** Once the bed comes home, ask your child to help you to take down the crib. This way, your child will feel part of the transition process and will also be able to say good-bye to the crib. Encouraging her to hold a toy screwdriver is sometimes enough to do the trick! Let your child help you set up her new bed and choose items she'd like to have in bed with her. Feel free to limit these items to one or two as having sixty-two stuffed animals in bed may be a bit stimulating in the middle of the night.

- **Step 5: Set up the bed.** Put the bed in a corner of your child's room so that the head and side of the bed are flush against the wall for protection. Add a safety rail to the exposed side of the bed. Your child will feel safely contained this way, just as he did in his crib.

- **Step 6: Explain the rules of bedtime.** If your child is verbal, before the first night of sleeping in the bed, go over the rules of bedtime with her. You could say, for example, "You'll be sleeping in your bed now, so we'll do our book, song, and snuggle, and then you will sleep in your bed all night long. Then, when the sun is nice and bright, you can let us know you're awake, and we'll come get you."

- **Step 7: Do your bedtime routine.** The first few nights your child is sleeping in his new bed, tack on an extra 10 or 15 minutes of reading time together, and include lots of holding and cuddling to help him settle into feeling comfortable. Also, make sure to play in the room during the day, if you don't do this already, to remind your child that his room is a place where he can feel safe and have fun and isn't just a place where he's separating from you.

If your child seems excited about the new bed and sleeps easily, you're one of those lucky people who has made this transition easily. If you're having a bumpy start, keep reading.

Sleeping in the Room with Your Child

If your child is having trouble transitioning from his crib to a bed, then one parent or the other (not both) can sleep in the room with him for a couple of nights. It's best not to start the habit of sleeping *in* bed with your child, but rather to set up a bed on the floor. Say to your child, "Mommy (or Daddy) is going to sleep with you in your room for a couple of nights to help you get used to sleeping in your new bed."

If your child pops out of bed as you're sleeping in there, simply return him to his bed and explain that he needs to sleep in his bed, and you'll sleep in yours. After the first couple of times, try to keep talking to a minimum, or don't talk at all, as doing so may continue to reinforce your child's getting out of bed. He may get out of bed lots of times the first night! Just continue to help him back each time.

You will have to go to sleep when your child does, and sleep in the room *all night long*. If he wakes up and finds that you're not there, he'll feel anxious about sleeping in his new bed, not to mention worried that he can't count on you doing what you say you will. Don't worry. You'll need to stay only a night or two—until your child is sleeping soundly through the night.

Leaving the Room

Once your child begins to sleep soundly through the night, you can experiment with trying to leave the room. On the first night that you're going to try to leave, tell your child during her bedtime routine that tonight, you're going to read and cuddle, and then she'll go to sleep in her bed and you'll sleep in your bed in the other room.

If your child protests and comes out of the room, walk her calmly back into her room, put her in her bed and leave the room quickly, saying "Good night, sweetie. Stay in bed now." If she continues to come out of the room, keep walking her back in consistently until she goes to sleep. She may try to come out fifty times, but she will eventually go to sleep *if you stay consistent.* Your consistent response will pay off because your child will realize there is no getting around the rule of staying in her bed. If your child sleeps through the night at that point, praise her the next day, make a big deal to important adults in her life that she did such a good job (grandparents, neighbors, teachers), and continue with the new routine the next night. She may test you again briefly, but she will soon learn to stay in bed and go to sleep.

If your child continues to protest by coming out of her room for several nights after you've left the room, follow the instructions in Chapter 3, "Step-by-Step Sleep."

Twins and Multiple Children
(Including Siblings of Different Ages)

It's hard enough to pour your heart and soul into one child, and having more than one requires every ounce of energy both you and your spouse have. The good news is that by having multiple children, you get the benefits of experiencing exponentially more joy. The not-so-good news is that you also experience exponentially more work. Without a doubt, there is very little room for sleep deprivation when you are parenting more than one child. Whether you have twins, triplets, or multi-aged siblings, you will need to do a little extra creative strategizing to bring good sleep into your household.

Twins

For simplicity, we'll refer to multiples as "twins" in this section, but if you have more than two, please try to generalize the information to your additional children. Also, as you help your children to sleep, please make sure that you are taking into account any prematurity and adjust their ages accordingly.

When twins first enter the world, it is appropriate and acceptable to have them sleep next to each other. After all, they've been "cosleeping" in the womb for nine months and will be comforted by continuing a similar sleep arrangement postpartum. It is a good idea to allow them to share a crib or other large sleep area and to get accustomed to the noises of their sibling early on so that they learn how to filter him out and get some sleep. Somewhere around 3 months, as the babies become more active, you may wish to separate them for sleep time and put each in his own crib. It should be fine to keep them in the same room, as they usually will be accustomed to tuning each other out. If one or both of your children seem especially sensitive to the other, however, you may want to use some white noise between their cribs for protection. Some parents of twins choose to keep their children in separate rooms because they have the space to do so and would rather not worry about one waking the other up. Either option is fine, as long as you're all able to sleep well.

When you have multiple children, scheduling plays an extremely important role in keeping you sane. Not only is it difficult to jump back and forth from child to child when their schedules are different, but it is extremely challenging when each child has his own timetable and you never get a break. To organize your children's sleep schedules, follow the instructions in Chapter 2, "Creating Your Child's Sleep Plan," with a few minor additions:

• If both of your children are having difficulty with sleep, begin to keep separate logs for each, tracking their daily and nightly schedules. Once you've tracked their typical day and night activities for about a week, including feedings, naps, sleep associations, and night wakings, take a look at your logs. If your children tend to wake each other up at night, you can decide whether you want to separate them for sleep learning. (We usually recommend doing so.) If you do need to separate them, put a playpen, crib, or bed in another room temporarily until both children are sleeping well, then reunite them again, using some white noise between their cribs or beds.

• Create Sleep Planners for each child according to current patterns, but keep the goal wake-up time in the morning the same for both so that they will each begin their day at the same time, nap together, and go to sleep at night simultaneously.

• If your spouse will be involved in working on sleep, assign one child to yourself and one to your spouse. You'll then each follow the instructions outlined in Chapter 3, "Step-by-Step Sleep."

• If your spouse is not available to help you with sleep learning and you don't have other support, plan on working with one child at a time, and then wait about a week before starting with the other child. Start with the child who has the most difficult issues first; once he is sleeping well you can begin working with the other.

* If one child wakes at the goal wake time (or at the end of at least a 1-hour nap) and the other is still sleeping, *wake the sleeping child* to keep the two of them on the same schedule. Keep both children awake until the next sleep period. To help them stay on the same schedule, always wake the child who wants to sleep longer, as long as each has gotten the appropriate amount of night or nap sleep.

* To juggle both children during the bedtime routine, if you don't have an additional pair of arms, use a bouncy chair or an exercise saucer to entertain a baby, or set up an older child with a puzzle or low-key activity.

Is It Okay to Wake a Sleeping Child?

It may seem counterintuitive to wake a sleeping child in the morning or from a nap because his twin has awoken earlier. When a child is progressing with his sleep skills, it's natural to want to reward him by letting him sleep according to his individual needs. However, if you do so, you risk having one child up and one child down, one child feeding while the other one is sleeping, and you'll never get a chance to leave the house or take a break.

Siblings

Parents who have multiple children of different ages usually want to improve sleep for each child but are concerned that the process will wake the other child up (translation: you'll have two screaming children in the middle of the night). As a result, these moms and dads have learned to jump at the first noise, especially if the children share a room.

For some families, their fear that one child will wake the other may be unfounded. Children who share rooms are often quite capable of sleeping through their sibling's wakings, especially in the middle of the night (and with a little bit of white noise for protection). You may want to try sleep learning for one night to see what happens. If it goes well, you may be able to keep your children together while they learn how to sleep.

Most often, though, we recommend separating kids for at least a few nights while parents work on sleep learning with one child. If parents are trying to help a younger baby sleep better, for instance, and the protest crying wakes her sibling, the older child may have difficulty at school or feel extremely cranky the next day. If you feel this is the likely scenario for your family, you can temporarily separate your children and put them back together when the baby is sleeping better. The best way to do this is to keep the child who is working on sleep in her familiar crib or bed while you move the good sleeper elsewhere. If your older child is verbal, ask him if he can be your "big helper" while you teach his baby sister how to sleep. Tell him he can sleep on a bed on the floor of your room while the baby learns. If you're worried that your older child will never be willing to *return* to his bed again once he gets a taste of your room, you can opt to move the baby into temporary separate quarters and leave your older child in his own room.

If both of your children are having sleep problems, then the advice outlined previously for multiples will apply to you, as well. (It's fine to help multiples sleep simultaneously—separating them temporarily—as long as there is one adult available to help each child.) However, kids of different ages will be on different schedules, especially during the day, so you can count on your younger child needing more frequent daytime sleep than your older child. If you have a preschooler and a baby, work with your baby first. When the baby starts to sleep better, praise her for a job well done (without overdoing it) in front of your preschooler. This tends to motivate the older child to perform well during sleep work.

Working Parents

For moms and dads who work, there are almost always some special concerns about sleep. Working can be extraordinarily difficult and heartrending for mothers because they tend to have more mixed emotions around separating during the day from their children. Whether you choose to stay at home, work part-time, or work full-time, there will always be gut-level conflict as you try to balance your needs with those of your child. For the purposes of this chapter, we will refer to a *mother* returning to work, although we are well aware that working and childrearing can be tough for dads, too.

If you've just returned to work and the separation from your baby feels terribly difficult, you are not alone. It is very hard, in the beginning, when you have been on maternity leave and are now handing over the reins of caregiving to another adult. There are often logistical changes for the baby or child in terms of where he spends his day (such as day care), and this alone will take some time to adjust to. Because they may feel guilty about leaving their child during the day, many parents find it difficult to maintain healthy sleep habits. They fear any boundaries will somehow deprive their child. Remember, though, that children desperately need good sleep nutrition. Make the most of your time together when your child is awake, and continue to protect his (and your) sleep.

Be sure to read the next two sections, "Adding Your Caregiver into the Picture" and "Working with Day Care," for information on how to collaborate on the changes in your child's sleep.

Making the Most of Your Time Together

Working parents can have a hard time balancing spending time with their child and protecting good sleep. Here are some ideas to help:

• Though it might be challenging to protect the bedtime if you don't get home until evening, try not to put your child down later than 8:30 PM (to avoid overfatigue).

• If you come home close to your child's bedtime, rather than spending time engaged in physical activity with your child, head right into the bedtime routine as your evening activity. Your child will love spending this quiet time with you.

Don't Begin Sleep Learning When You First Return to Work

Your first few weeks back at work are not an ideal time to start sleep learning. Instead, give yourself and your child some time to adjust. Once you're all feeling more comfortable with the changes, you may then begin to work on sleep.

Start Sleep Learning on the Weekend

We often recommend that working parents begin sleep learning on the weekend, when they can spend some extra time with their child. Doing so will help alleviate any guilt that comes from leaving during the day and setting loving limits at nighttime.

Adding Your Caregiver into the Picture

If you have a caregiver but don't work out of the home, it's best that *you* help your child make changes with sleep rather than asking your caregiver to do so. You hired your caregiver to take care of your child, and she may not feel comfortable setting the same limits you need to set. Also, you don't want to risk all of your hard work going down the drain due to lack of consistency.

If you work out of the home, however, your caregiver will indeed be the point person for helping your child make changes with naps, so it's important to explain to your caregiver exactly how to prepare your child for sleep (including detailed information about the bedtime routine), stressing the importance of putting him down *awake*. Go over how to do check-ins, as well as the possible scenarios that will ensue as your child learns how to nap (see Chapter 5, "The Art of the Nap"; you might also ask your caregiver to read that chapter as well as Chapter 3, "Step-by-Step Sleep"). Write down your child's schedule, and explain how to time naps. Allow plenty of time for questions and discussion, and be patient; it may take your caregiver time to adjust to the new changes, routines, and schedule. Lastly, ask her to jot down details about how your child slept during the day (and how much he ate) so you'll know how to plan for nighttime sleep.

Ask your caregiver to provide feedback on how she's feeling during the sleep-learning process. If she has any questions or concerns, address them immediately. Let your caregiver know how important it is that she support your child's good sleep skills. If she cannot follow your instructions, you may want to give her a pep talk and speak from the depths of your heart about how important sleep is to your whole family. If she is inconsistent with the plan you've used to help your child sleep at night, she will inadvertently unravel the progress you've made.

Working with Day Care

At some day care facilities, providers are happy to put children down awake (after you've already taught your child how to nap well) and to adhere to scheduling guidelines. Others are much stricter about sleep rules and may be unwilling to bend. Be sure to talk to your day care provider before you begin working on sleep to ensure that your child will be able to continue her good skills in day care. If possible, take some time off of work to help your child nap well at home; then transition her back to the day care environment gradually. Be sure to outline your new wind-down routine; if necessary (and possible), bring white noise to help your child sleep in a potentially noisy environment.

Parenting on Your Own

Parenting with a spouse is hard enough. When you are a single parent, the job becomes exponentially more difficult. Not only do you have the additional burdens of doing *all* of the caregiving, decision making, and financial supporting, but it can be nearly impossible to feel like you have time to take care of yourself. Nonetheless, because you are the main source for meeting your child's needs (grandparents and other helpers count, too, but no one replaces you), taking care of yourself becomes vitally important when you're a single parent.

Add to these monumental demands a sleep problem, and you have a recipe for fast burnout. When a single parent is sleep deprived, the family's well-being hangs in the balance even more critically than when there are two parents. Please don't hesitate to ask for extra support. Even once your sleep problem is resolved, you'll have the daily logistical juggle of child care, dinner and bedtime preparations. Who can help? It may be wise to consider, if possible, a revolving arsenal of different people—family members, friends, day care providers, or hired help. Maybe you and a friend can take turns watching each other's child every so often.

You'll also want to try to prioritize what is absolutely necessary and what will have to fall by the wayside. Obviously, eating, sleeping, working, and caring for your child are top priorities; if the vacuum gathers its own dust in the closet or it takes you a whole week to return phone calls, try to give yourself a break. You're doing the best you can, and there is only so much of you to go around. But even if it seems like an impossible task, try to schedule in *something* for yourself a couple of times a week—maybe a walk to the neighborhood coffee shop or lunch with a friend. Include your child if you don't have the option of leaving her with anyone, but once in a while try to do things without her, too. As a single parent, it's easy to feel guilty about taking a break. But you're not doing your child any favors by refusing to refuel; she can sense your exhaustion and overwhelmed state, and your bond will only grow if you're both excited to spend time together. She'll delight in your refreshed mood.

Traveling

You would think that any family who's worked their tushes off to get great sleep would deserve a little vacation. We're certainly not here to argue. You do deserve it! We hope you're going somewhere fun and relaxing and away from it all.

But . . . yes, there's a "but." The truth is that not all children travel well. Some are incredibly flexible and just adapt to the new environment and new time zone without batting an eye. (If you have one of these amazing children, be careful about bragging too much; some jealous parent might switch your suitcase for one filled with sand.) Many others, though, really don't like being away from home sweet home that much. They get confused or scared by the new surroundings, and their bodies feel tired from traveling. They resist going to sleep, or they wake throughout the night, crying. Suddenly, your great little sleeper at home can become your worst little nightmare away from home. There are several things you can do, though, to ensure that your travel will go as smoothly as possible.

Getting There

Try to schedule travel—whether a flight or car trip—during a nap time or around your child's bedtime. Yep, sometimes red-eye flights might be the way to go. Hopefully, your child will then be able to sleep on the way and not be extremely overtired by the time you get to your destination. The other benefit of a night flight is that your child will not get too bogged down with boredom being strapped into his seat for too long before it's time for some shut-eye.

For an older child, be sure to pack several sippy cups or juice boxes with favorite beverages (but beware the cranberry or grape juice that will stain clothing or seats); easy, no-mess snacks (bite-size crackers, string cheese, and deli meat tend to work well—skip the fruit); and new toys that will be sure to entertain your child because he's never played with them before and will occupy him longer. If you're driving a long distance, make frequent stops for the bathroom, or just to stretch legs and release some pent-up energy. It also may be wise to carry along all of your child's goofy CDs, painful as that may be.

If you're traveling by plane, you may want to spend the extra money to invest in a separate seat for your child (sometimes airlines offer these seats at discounted rates). Doing so is not only an important protective measure for her safety—you'll be able to buckle her in for take-off and landing—but it will also give your arms a break, particularly on a long flight. For take-off and landing, plan to help your child drink some liquid; offer breast or bottle for babies, sippy cup with water or juice for older children. Swallowing continuously at these times will help prevent pressure from building in her ears and protect them from discomfort. Just make sure to wait until you actually hear the plane engine rev loudly as it begins its roar down the runway before you begin to give breast or bottle. Many parents make the mistake of offering their baby a whole feeding while the plane backs out of the gate, only to find that there are twelve other planes in line for takeoff. By the time the baby really needs to swallow, she's stuffed! For landing, the most difficult part on the ears is actually the beginning descent and not the final touch down. Once your pilot makes the announcement that you are dropping in elevation, and your own ears begin to feel a bit stuffy, that's the time to begin to offer your child fluids.

You might find that your child is nervous or upset on the flight—or her ears may bother her despite your precautions. Translation: she might begin to wail the minute you take off and refuse to let up till the moment the wheels touch down. We've all been on public transportation—plane, train, bus—with a screaming child. (We have a theory that if you *were* once that screaming child, then karma will ensure that there's always one in your vicinity while traveling. True confessions: one of us has that karma, but we're not telling who!) It's not your fault. It's not her fault. Ignore the evil stares of the passengers around you and do the best you can; walk her around, sing her some songs, keep trying liquids or a snack. Flight attendants are often very sympathetic to children who get upset on flights and might even have a trick or two up their sleeves to help calm her down. Even if she doesn't, remember: this too shall pass.

Creating a Good Sleep Environment

If your child is still in a crib, arrange for a crib at your destination, if possible. (Call in advance to ensure that it meets all safety regulations.) If it isn't possible to get a crib, bring a portable playpen. If you are using a crib, bring a crib sheet from home that you haven't washed in a few days, so it smells familiar to your child. Also bring whatever else he is currently attached to: blankies, stuffed animals, pacifiers, favorite toys or books, favorite pj's.

When you arrive at your destination, spend some time with your child in the room where he'll be sleeping to help him orient to that space. Play with him there; unpack while he's amusing himself on the floor. Tell him this will be his room for a while and show him his crib or bed. Bring white noise with you to protect your child against unusual sounds in the new environment, like the clickety-clack of the room service cart in the hallway.

If you're in a hotel, blackout shades are almost always par for the course. If you'll be in someone's home, though, either bring materials with you to darken the windows (black plastic garbage bags work well, even if they don't look so hot), or graciously ask your hosts to secure these for you. The dark windows will help your child sleep till his scheduled wake time and take good naps.

Dealing with Time Zone Changes

If you're traveling west to east, deciding whether to keep your child on the same time zone as home or not will really depend on a couple of factors. First, how long are you staying where you're going? If it's more than a week, it's going to be pretty tough to keep your child on the same old time zone, as her body will more than likely begin to adjust on its own from sunlight.

If you're going east for *under* a week, however, you may be able to stay on the same time schedule as the one you'll be returning to. We call this "vacation schedule"—your child will stay up later at night, then sleep later in the morning (and so will you!). So, for example, if you live in Denver and are traveling to New York (New York time is 2 hours later than Denver), and your child normally goes to bed at 7:30 PM and wakes at 6:30 AM, by the clock she'll now go to sleep at 9:30 PM and wake at 8:30 AM. You can allow her to nap at the later times, too. If your child automatically wakes when Mr. Sun does, just roll with it and follow the directions below for when you travel home.

If you're traveling east to west, it's a bit trickier. Your child will inevitably wake early the first day; you really don't have a choice but to get up with her. Then, watch the clock. You're going to try to s-t-r-e-t-c-h her as far as you can toward her regular nap time, according to the time zone you're in. So, for example, if you're traveling from Miami to Los Angeles (Los Angeles time is 3 hours earlier than Miami), and your 18-month-old child normally goes to bed at 8:00 PM and wakes at 7:00 AM, she may wake at 4:00 AM the first morning (ouch!). If she normally naps at 11:30 AM, try to stretch her as far toward that time by the current clock as you can; 11:30 will feel like 2:30 in the afternoon, though, so she'll never make it all the way there the first day. The first day, you might have her nap at, say, 9:00 AM (and then you'd try for a second shorter nap, perhaps in a car or stroller, later in the day to tide her over to bedtime). That night, you're again going to s-t-r-e-t-c-h her as far as you can toward bedtime by the current clock, but given that 8:00 PM will now feel like 11:00, she might make it only till 6:30 the first night (which will feel like 9:30).

Then, the next morning, help her stretch again with her wake time; when she wakes early, try doing a check-in or two (if she's not crying hard, or if you're in an environment where you would feel comfortable allowing a bit of crying), or try laying a hand on her and reassuring her with your soft voice: "Shhh, sweetie, it's not time to get up yet! I'll come get you when it's time." In reality, she may not be able to go back to sleep, as her body's biorhythms are adjusting to the time change. But as long as you continue the "stretch" toward each sleep period for the next couple of days, you should arrive at a livable schedule.

Helping Your Child Sleep Away from Home

When it's time for bed, do as much of your usual wind-down routine as you possibly can. The first couple of nights are the most important in terms of ensuring consistency. Thereafter, do as much of it as you can given that you're on vacation. For instance, you might skip the bath, but you'll still do the feed and the book if that's what you do at home.

Do the best you can with naps. You'll probably be on the go a lot during the day, so if your child falls asleep in the stroller or car, it's okay to allow this. If he doesn't, try not to skip too many naps in a row, or he'll be overtired by the time nighttime comes.

Plan to spend an extra 10 or 15 minutes helping your child wind down before sleep the first couple of nights, to help him relax and feel safe in the new environment. If your child should wake in the night, go to him—this isn't the time to let him cry, as he may legitimately be feeling afraid. Start with the most minimal assistance: try doing a check-in, using your voice and presence only, and see if he'll go back to sleep. If another minute or two goes by and he's still upset, go to him and rub his tummy (or his back, for an older child), and calm him down: "Shhh, sweetie, it's okay, I'm right here." If *that* doesn't work after another minute or two, pick your child up, hold him, comfort him . . . and try to put him back down awake. If all else fails, help your child to sleep. Feed him, rock him, pull him into bed with you if you have to. *And don't worry about it.* In this situation, your assistance is appropriate. The minute you get home, you'll come right back to your nice sleep foundation—your predictable bedtime routine, down awake, check-ins as needed for a night or two perhaps. Don't worry, it shouldn't feel like you're starting over—remember, he knows how to ride that bike, and he may be wobbly at first but he'll quickly regain his confidence.

Daylight Saving Time

For better or for worse, twice a year most of us are subject to a time change. This can influence your child's sleep either positively or negatively, but either way it forces you to make a shift in the carefully constructed schedule you've worked so hard to create for your child.

Spring Ahead

Here are some tips to help you spring ahead without falling behind on sleep:

Before you go to bed, turn your clocks ahead 1 hour. If your child normally sleeps till 6:30 AM, the next morning she will likely sleep until 7:30 AM (which still feels like 6:30 to her). If you are happy about this change, great! Just protect her room from too much light entering in the early morning, and use white noise so she won't wake with the birds. If you'd rather help your child get back to her usual schedule, however, try the following:

1. Put your child down at her regular bedtime, say 7:30 PM, on Saturday night.

2. Set your alarm for 6:30 AM (according to the new clock) and *wake your child* at this time. It will feel to her body like it's actually 5:30 AM, but don't worry. She'll be a bit tired today, but she will adjust.

3. If your child naps, put her down at her normal nap time according to the new clock and resume your normal schedule from there. Don't allow your child to nap longer than she usually does.

4. On Sunday night, put her down at her usual bedtime according to the new time.

Fall Back

This is the time change that most parents dread. Just as they're heading into the colder months, parents now also have to contend with the fact that their child will be waking 1 hour earlier once the clocks have changed. To ensure that the shift goes as smoothly as possible:

1. Put your child to sleep at his normal bedtime on Saturday night.

2. Your child will likely wake up 1 hour earlier by the new clock than he normally does, say at 5:00 AM (which still feels to his body like 6:00 AM). Psychologically, it can be painful to see 5:00 AM on your clock and deal with a child who's feeling bright and perky, even though you've all gotten the usual amount of sleep. There's not a whole lot you can do about his energy level on this first morning, so just get up with him.

3. If your child is still taking naps, stretch him as much as you can toward his normal first nap time (according to the current clock),

even if he's tired. In other words, if your child wakes at 5:00 AM
(according to the current clock), his body will probably want to
nap 1 hour earlier than normal. Don't let him! Instead, do anything and everything to keep him awake. Put him in the bath
to splash around or do the Hokey Pokey around your living
room to make sure he stays up as close to his normal first nap
time as possible. Then follow, as closely as you can, his usual
schedule thereafter. Don't let him nap too long, as doing so may
continue to cause early morning wakings.

If your child is old enough to have outgrown napping, you will still
need to allow him to wake up at the early new time once the clocks
have been changed (bummer). However, spend your day eating and
doing activities according to the usual time (even though the clock
has changed), then do your best to keep him up all the way until his
regular bedtime at night, by the new clock. Yes, he'll be a bit cranky
in the evening, but after a few days, he'll adjust. Remember, spring-
time *will* return in about six months!

Moving

Moving from one home to another is a big transition for the whole
family. For parents, it's simply a ton of work and planning, and it's
hard to have a little one interrupting you repeatedly for something or
another when you're trying to pack. From a child's perspective, moving causes Mommy and Daddy to be stressed out and less available,
and a change in her environment can feel very strange to her at first.

Depending on her age, there are a variety of ways to help ease your
child's transition. Moving is not as complicated for a baby under 5
months as it is for an older child. This is because younger babies do

not recognize their environment as clearly as older children do. Maintaining familiarity in loveys, favorite toys, or in the smell of their *unwashed* crib sheet may be enough to get your baby through the change easily. It is also helpful to create a cozy bedroom environment for your child as quickly as possible. If you use any white noise or room darkening shades, try to set these up before attempting the first go at sleep. It is also especially important to use your nighttime or nap time routine before putting your baby into her crib for the first few times. The bedtime routine alone can go a long way toward helping her sleep comfortably.

For older babies, toddlers, and preschoolers, the situation looks a little bit different. Even an 8-month-old baby has grown accustomed to his home environment, and when that changes, he may be a bit thrown off for a day or two. Consider some of the following suggestions:

- Prior to the big move, try to visit your new home with your child. If he isn't verbal yet, allow him to carefully explore his new room, and tell him that this will be his special space once you move in. For an older child, it can be helpful to make a small book about the move and to include pictures of his new room and the house. (For more on making books, please see the section in Chapter 9 entitled "Creating Books to Help Ease Transitions.") If you'd like, ask him how he might want to fix up his new room or bed. If you're reluctant to hand over the decorating power to your preschooler, shop together for a special new pillowcase or a special item for his new room.

- Before you even unpack your own toothbrush, try to set up your child's room as much as you can. If possible, try to re-create the look of her old room so that she will feel some sense of familiarity. If you've decided to trash all of her old furnishings and go nuts with the credit card, put some old favorite toys or her lovey in her room so that she feels more at home.

- Do your familiar bedtime routine, just as you always have. If your child seems afraid to go to sleep, you may want to set up a bed on the floor near his crib or bed and tell him that you will stay close by the first couple of nights as he adjusts to his new room.

- Make sure to play with your child in her room frequently during the day so she begins to develop a fondness for her new surroundings.

Bumps in the Road

Imagine this: you work very hard for a few nights to follow your sleep plan 100 percent consistently. To your complete delight and amazement, your child begins sleeping through the night and taking good naps. At first you don't quite believe it; "It can't last," you think. "It's too good to be true." But it does last, and the more rest your child gets, the happier and more alert he seems. And the more rest *he* gets, the more *you* get—and you're much happier, too. After a few days, or even weeks, of enjoying wonderful, peaceful, restful sleep, you begin to feel like you've reached nirvana.

Then, suddenly, *whammo!* Your child gets sick or begins cutting a tooth. Or she takes her first steps. Or you take a trip or have visitors in your home. Suddenly, everything's upside-down again. Your child is having a hard time settling down, waking at night, or resisting naps . . . all over again. *What happened?*

Life happened. Kids are human beings, and they sometimes get sick. They grow and change. Your life together will take twists and turns. And inevitably, your child's newfound great sleep habits will be compromised when circumstances beyond anyone's reasonable control affect her ability to sleep well. Even the most perfect sleeper will not be able to sleep well when she's not feeling well or when she's jetlagged or when she's just begun to walk.

Fear not. Just because these bumps are inevitable doesn't mean they have to last long—*if you stay committed* to helping your child come right back to her good sleep foundation once the crisis or temporary situation has passed.

What follows are many of the scenarios you'll encounter that will likely affect your child's sleep, and how to handle each one. If you can make peace with the fact that it's not a matter of *whether* your child's sleep will be affected at some point but *when*, you'll be much less likely to panic when the time comes. And just as we helped you get on track with sleep in the first place, we'll help you get back on track, too. We wouldn't leave you in the middle of a sleep crisis!

Q: Our child has been sleeping well for several months since he learned how to sleep, but now he's been sick for a week. We're up with him all night, almost every hour; it feels like we're right back where we started.

A: If only we could put a protective bubble around our children and prevent them from experiencing anything that would ever disrupt their sleep again! You worked *so hard* to finally get good sleep in your household, so of course you don't look forward to feeling like you have to start over again.

When your child is sick, you absolutely must go to him at night or during naps when he cries and do *whatever it takes* to help him— feed, cuddle, rock, or lie down together. Then, when the symptoms have faded and he's feeling better, it's time to return to good sleep habits. When a child's sleep has been disrupted—whether due to illness, teething, hitting a milestone, or travel—you will have to help him get back on track by returning to your predictable sleep-time routines and putting him down awake, then using your check-ins if he wakes in the night. But it really shouldn't be like starting over. Learning how to sleep is like learning how to ride a bike. Sometimes that bike will sit in the shed for a few days, even a week or so, but your child still knows how to ride that bike even if he's taken a break from it. He might be a little wobbly at first, but with your help and support he'll remember what to do soon.

Q: What if I had weaned my nighttime feedings while sleep learning, and then began feeding my child again while she was sick or teething?

A: If you've only been feeding for a couple of days, and your child is older than 6 months, you don't have to worry about weaning. If your child is 4 to 6 months or you want to be conservative, you can offer her 1 ounce or 1 minute less than the most you've been offering, then subtract 1 to 2 ounces or minutes over a series of successive nights until the feeds are weaned away again.

If you've been feeding your child for more than a week, and she is less than 12 months old, simply follow the weaning instructions in Chapter 2.

Q: We think our child is cutting a tooth. How should we handle this?

A: The first thing to do is to make sure that the culprit is actually teething. If your child has been sleeping well and has suddenly begun waking with a sharp-sounding cry (usually an indication of pain), look for some of the symptoms of acute teething (for more on this, please see "Problem: Teething" in Chapter 7). If you see none, then it probably isn't his teeth that are causing pain; your child may be sick (note that ear infections are particularly difficult to self-diagnose, as it's hard to see symptoms). Consult your pediatrician, who can determine the source of your child's discomfort.

If your child is actively cutting a tooth, you can, with your doctor's permission, offer pain reliever about 30 minutes before bedtime; if your child wakes throughout the night, go to him immediately and do whatever you can to help comfort and soothe him. (You can even feed him if you'd like, but if you've already weaned nighttime feeds, try to soothe him in other ways first, such as by holding or rocking him. If you offer milk for only a few nights, you do not need to rewean your feeds.)

Once the tooth cuts through the gum, your child's pain significantly diminishes, and his mood and behavior should return to normal. At that point, help your child return to his good sleep foundation, putting him down awake and doing check-ins (or walking him back to bed) as needed. Usually, it doesn't take much to get a child back on track after a bout of teething, since he won't have been off track for long.

Q: **Just when we got to the end of sleep learning and our child was finally sleeping through the night, she began crawling for the first time. Now she won't nap, and she's waking early. Help!**

A: We've often noticed that once children finally begin to get the rest they need, their brains and bodies suddenly have enough fuel to catapult forward developmentally. This is a good news–bad news situation; the good news is that she's achieved a new milestone. The bad news is that just after you got her sleep settled into a nice pattern, she started waking again.

You should still continue with your predictable bedtime routines and putting her to sleep on time. Most babies won't wake throughout the night when they begin doing something new with their bodies, though some may due to separation anxiety. You'll have to settle for some early mornings for a few days until you've noticed her excitement about her new skills begin to fade. If she's not napping well, you'll also want to take a break on naps—either settle for shorter naps, temporarily, and put her down more frequently, or use motion (car, stroller, or swing) to help her take longer naps. Anywhere from a few days to a week or two after she's hit the milestone (crawling and walking are the most exciting), when you've noticed her excitement subside during the day, you can return to your sleep plan. It shouldn't be like starting all over again, but you may have another night or two of some check-ins to help her get back on track.

Q: After a couple of days of sleep learning, we thought we were in the home stretch—our child was going down with little or no crying, and if she woke she put herself back to sleep fairly quickly. Then she suddenly started waking at night again. She's not sick or teething, and she hasn't just hit a new developmental milestone. What happened?

A: This phenomenon has a clinical term, and it's called an *extinction burst*. It can happen on the third night, the fifth, or really at any point as you're helping your child learn how to sleep, and it can feel like suddenly all your hard work has gone out the window. All it means is that your child is in the final stages of learning how to sleep, and that her old behavior is returning *briefly* for one final curtain call before bowing out for good. Although it can feel disheartening to have a bumpy night after several much smoother ones, rest assured that her new sleep habits have indeed begun to solidify, and she'll probably sleep much better the very next night.

Q: As we started to do sleep learning, my child began to climb out of his crib. What do we do?

A: Some children, as they begin to protest changes around sleep, attempt to climb out of the crib. Your child's safety takes priority over sleep, so here are a few suggestions for how to handle this potentially very dangerous situation:

- Lower the mattress to the lowest possible setting, and make sure you have removed bumpers and all toys (except transitional objects) that your child might be able to stand on and get leverage.

- If you see your child beginning to climb or if he has already climbed out but has not hurt himself, say to him firmly, "No climbing," put him back in the crib, and leave the room. Arrange pillows and other items around your child's crib in the event that he does try to climb again that night.

- If your child continues to climb out of the crib after having been told several times not to do so, you have two options. One is to use a mesh crib tent, which attaches to the crib and provides a breathable protective cover; the other is to transition to a bed. Either option will work as long as you are committed to it. The crib tent works well for many families; others feel that it is too confining for their child.

- If you decide to use a crib tent, suspend sleep learning until you have purchased the tent and installed it properly. Then continue with your sleep plan.

If you do decide to transition your child to a bed, stop sleep learning and follow the instructions in "Transitioning Your Child from a Crib to a Bed" earlier in this chapter. Make sure your child is comfortable in the bed before you begin sleep learning.

Q: It's been two weeks since we taught our child to sleep, and she still cries for 10 to 15 minutes when I put her down for bedtime or for a nap. Is this normal?

A: It's considered normal for a child to spend up to 15 minutes settling herself into sleep, whether at nighttime or for a nap. Some children just need to discharge energy as they wind down, and crying is their way of doing so.

That having been said, your child may also be slightly overtired by the time you are putting her down. See what happens if you shave 15 minutes off of the bedtime or nap time. If your child still cries the same amount of time, then crying is just her way of settling. But if she cries less or not at all, you'll want to adjust the timing permanently.

Also, make sure that her room is very dark and that there aren't any ambient sounds that may be disrupting her. If you discover one, use white noise.

Q: It seems impossible to keep my 4-month-old baby awake for 2 hours after she wakes for the day or 2½ hours between her naps. I'm also not having much luck stretching her naps to an hour. What should I do?

A: Some babies are not ready to stretch their waketime windows during the day to the intervals we discuss in Chapter 5 until closer to 4½ months. These babies may also not be able to sleep more than 45 minutes for a nap. In this case, you can allow your baby to take her first nap 1½ hours after she wakes for the day, then put her down every 2 hours for the rest of the day. In other words, your baby will probably take four naps rather than three. Once your baby is 4½ months old, though, try to stretch her the additional half hour per waketime interval to help her consolidate her nap sleep.

Q: My child is taking three naps a day, and sometimes I run out of time to squeeze in the third nap. For instance, he usually sleeps from 8:30 to 10:00 AM, then from 12:30 to 2:30 PM. Another 2½ hours would be 5:00 PM, but that seems awfully late for a nap.

A: When your baby gets the bulk of his daytime sleep during his first two naps—3 hours or more—then he won't need much for his third nap; a short "blip" of 15 to 30 minutes will suffice. It's perfectly fine to use motion for the third nap—car or stroller works well, if your child will sleep this way (it's fine to put him in the crib, as well). Babies under 8 months can usually sleep *until* about 4:30 or 5:00 PM and still go down to sleep on time for bedtime, at say 7:00 or 7:30 PM, but experiment with your child; if he sleeps this late and then seems quite alert at his normal bedtime, you'll have to wake him earlier from the third nap.

So for the example given in the question, you could take your child out at around 5:00, waking him by 5:15 or 5:20 PM, then adjust the bedtime later by 15 or 20 minutes that evening. If this situation occurs frequently, your child may be ready for two naps a day, in which case you can help him stretch his daytime wake windows by a half hour and temporarily adjust the bedtime earlier to help him stretch from the end of the second nap until bedtime without becoming overtired. Alternatively, you can try shortening the second nap by a half hour to allow enough time at the end of the day for a third short nap.

Q: My child's naps were going fine, and suddenly she's crying (or talking) as I put her down in the crib. What's going on?

A: Always begin by looking for "the big four": illness, teething, hitting a motor milestone, or recent travel or visitors. (Additionally, if you have an older child, assess whether she's working through an emotional issue, such as starting preschool or adjusting to a new baby.) If you suspect or are certain that your child is dealing with any of these issues, please see previous sections on these issues specifically.

If you've ruled out these issues and you're certain that she's not hungry or in discomfort, or that there are any environmental issues standing in her way (such as loud sounds in the household or neighborhood), consider adjusting the timing of her naps. Is she a bit more tired than she used to be going down for the nap? If so, adjust the naptime earlier by 15 minutes and see how she does. Conversely, does she suddenly seem more alert and awake at nap time than she used to (perhaps because she's beginning to catch up on sleep and can now stay awake a bit longer between naps)? If this is the case, try adjusting the nap time later by 15 or 30 minutes.

Q: My child's scheduled feeding falls right in the middle of a nap. How do I handle this?

A: It is very common, especially for those children who are still napping three times a day, for a feeding to be due right in the middle of a nap. We advise parents to stick to the right *timing* of naps and offer the baby a little "tank up" feed prior to nap time to help hold him until he wakes up. You can then go ahead and offer him scheduled feedings thereafter, but again, if your child is due for a second or third nap, you can always offer a bit of milk prior to putting him down, so he won't awaken from a nap due to hunger.

Q: Although my child's sleep has improved significantly, he seems more tired than ever. Why?

A: Once children are sleeping better, it is not at all uncommon for them to look a bit tired and want to go back to sleep frequently. If you think about it, this makes a lot of sense. They have quite a bit of catching up to do on snooze hours once they learn how to get them. You may also feel this way for quite some time. You finally can allow your body to relax into deep sleep, and your body may scream *"more"* until it feels rejuvenated. Don't worry, you will all soon feel more rested, and these signs of exhaustion will go away.

Q: I have a toddler and a baby, and I'm the only one available to put them both down at night—my spouse doesn't get home from work until

later. My toddler has lots of energy, and when I try to settle the baby in her room, my older child starts running around and laughing loudly. What can I do?

A: The age of your toddler has a lot to do with how you can best handle this situation. If your child is verbal and is able to regulate his impulses at all, you can tell him that you need to put the baby down, and after you do, you and he can have "special time." Tell him that if he interrupts you too much or makes too much noise, it will take you longer to put the baby to sleep, and you won't have a chance to play together before bed. You can ask him to make a choice: "Would you like to have special time with Mommy?" (We're imagining he'd like that very much!) "Can you make a choice? Either you can stay nice and quiet and read a book here, and then we'll go have our special time, or you can go play quietly with your trains in your room until Mommy comes in." (Make sure your child will remain safe on his own.) Ask him, "What's your choice?" When given some control over the situation, your toddler is more likely to be better behaved. The key is to follow through on your consequences here. If he continues to make noise and interrupt you, tell him, "Uh-oh . . . I guess we don't have enough time for special playing together! We'll have to try again tomorrow," and proceed to put him to bed without any special time.

If your child is not yet old enough to understand much explanation, you may need to use some special props to keep him occupied while you're putting the baby down. You may need to save up your "video babysitter" for just this moment, when having two little ones is too much to handle at the same time. You can also put your child in his room with a safety gate at the door, tell him you'll be right back, and give him some highly entertaining toys and some fun background music while you move through the baby's routine as quickly as possible.

It is for this very reason that second, third, and fourth children are not often the recipients of lengthy, elaborate bedtime routines like their older siblings were. Somehow, with brief activities as simple as changing the diaper and putting on pj's, doing a feeding, and singing one verse of "Twinkle, Twinkle Little Star," these kids wind up just fine.

Helping your baby to become independent in her ability to fall asleep will go a long way in getting you back to your toddler as quickly as possible!

Q: Help! No matter what I do, my child still wakes early.

A: Early morning wakings are one of the toughest sleep problems to fix—if not *the* toughest. Why? Because after a decent night's rest, he's got more energy to fight sleep in the morning; in addition, all of us come up into lighter sleep phases in the last hour of our sleep, preparing to wake up for the day. Remember, though, your child is waking early *only* if he is not getting the right amount of night rest for his age and his body. In other words, if your child sleeps from 7 PM to 6 AM, although this may feel early to you, it's a perfectly reasonable schedule for him. We can't ask children to sleep more than the minimum of 11 hours at night; their bodies are usually rested after this much sleep, and they won't be able to do more.

Remember also that if your child is waking even at 10½ hours, if he is rested and energetic in the morning *and* makes it easily till his naptime, then he's getting enough rest *for his body*. This is particularly challenging if your child sleeps from, say, 7 PM to 5:30 AM. In this case, you can experiment with pushing the bedtime later by 15-minute increments, then watching to see if your child can sleep later in the morning. Be warned: making the bedtime later can often have the *opposite* effect of causing your child to wake up earlier. This is why it's important to make changes in small steps.

Here are some other ideas to try to help with early morning wakings:

- Make certain that your child's room is extremely dark (9 to 10 on a scale of 10, 10 being dark). Tack up a heavy blanket, poster board, or garbage bags if necessary.

- If there are any sounds that could be waking him—such as one parent showering, garbage trucks, sprinklers, or a barking dog—put white noise in the room (use an appliance or purchase a white noise machine) and make the volume loud enough to protect him from these sounds.

- Remove all stimulating toys from your child's crib or bed, which can be distracting once the sun comes into his room.

- If you are checking in on your child within the last hour before his wake time, the interaction with him may prevent him from returning to sleep. Consider not checking in if it's less than 60 minutes till his wake time, or consider stretching your check-in intervals much wider at this time.

- Make sure the bedtime is not too late for your child's age. Adjust the bedtime earlier by 15-minute increments, and watch what happens in the morning. Often, doing so will allow your child to sleep later, as he is less overtired at bedtime; if he does wake earlier, however, return to your previous bedtime. If moving the bedtime earlier has no effect on the wake time, you may want to consider using the earlier bedtime anyway to help your child get the right amount of night sleep for his age.

- Assess whether your child is doing something new with his body (such as crawling or walking), experiencing another kind of developmental burst (such as increased language), dealing with a new situation (such as a new baby in the home or starting preschool), or adjusting to a time change. If any of these conditions are present, you'll need to settle for the early waking temporarily (see the developmental chapter for your child's age as well as the previous sections of this chapter that address travel and time changes).

• Make sure that your child is not hungry. If you have a child under 12 months and have newly begun to wean feedings, you may want to slow the process down a bit to give him more time to adjust. Be careful also to ensure that you are offering the breast or bottle more often during the day to help him transition his previous nighttime feeds to the daytime, so he won't be hungry going down for sleep at night.

• For older, verbal children, you can try writing the wake up time on a piece of paper (example: 6:00) and taping it above a digital clock. Tell him that when the numbers on the paper match the clock, he can get out of bed. Alternatively, you can have the clock play music at his designated wake up time, signaling that it's okay to get out of bed.

CONCLUSION: From Our Hearts to Yours

Whew! What a lot of information you've just digested. Take a deep breath. It can seem overwhelming to think about making changes with your child's sleep, and right now you're standing at the bottom of the mountain looking up. Rest assured, though, that thousands of families have used these exact same methods, and—with consistency—have begun to enjoy that view from the top after only a few nights. What does that view look like? Your child goes down each and every night on time with very little or no crying, sleeps soundly through the night, and takes regular naps at the same time each day. Sounds good, doesn't it?

If you follow our methods carefully, you, too, can help your family to become well rested. Your hard work on sleep really pays off when you see the positive impact good sleep nutrition has on your attachment with your child and spouse. A rested child is a thriving child, and his mood, behavior, and physical capabilities will all improve. You become better able to parent effectively and lovingly, and your relationship with your spouse becomes stronger. In the long run, what's most important in families is that each member has energy and love to give to one another.

When your child does begin sleeping well and has had a week or two to solidify her new abilities, you can ease up a bit on the strictness of your scheduling and timing. Now you'll get some flexibility back—there will be times when you'll want to have dinner at a friend's house past your child's bedtime or run errands as a family on the weekend at nap time. It's okay to balance family needs with what your child needs! Just make sure that in the big picture, your child continues to put herself to sleep independently and gets the proper amount of sleep overall.

You are giving your child and your family a tremendous gift by ensuring that you all get a good night's sleep. So here's to getting lots of good shut-eye, and we look forward to hearing your stories of success!

Sleep Planner: For Crib Sleepers

A. Bedtime Routine Checklist

Put a check next to the activities you would like to do each night. Then write a number next to each one, so you can remember to do them in the same order every time.

___ ☐ Bath

___ ☐ Diaper and pj's

___ ☐ Milk

___ ☐ Quiet play on the floor (no stimulating toys)

___ ☐ Rocking

___ ☐ Story or books (including the one you make together about changes at bedtime, for a verbal child)

___ ☐ Singing or music

___ ☐ Favorite ritual (such as saying good night to stuffed animals
or the moon)

___ ☐ Turning on white noise

___ ☐ Offering lovey, "Mommy Bear," or other transitional object

___ ☐ Cuddling before leaving the room

___ ☐ Other: _____

_____

B. My Child's Sleep Associations

Write down the associations your child may have with falling asleep, such as sucking, motion, or lying down with a parent.

1. _____
2. _____
3. _____
4. _____
5. _____

C. Environmental Checklist

Use this checklist to get your child's sleeping space ready to begin sleep learning. If you don't have the environment quite right, *don't start sleep learning!* You want to give your child every possible chance to sleep well.

1. **Remove stimulating or unsafe items from inside and around the crib.**

☐ Toys

☐ Mobile

☐ Aquariums/music boxes

☐ Bumpers (if child can pull to a stand)

☐ Blankets

☐ Other items in or near your child's crib that may be stimulating

2. **Make room dark** (on a scale of 10, if 10 is dark, go for 8 or 9!).

   ☐ Install room-darkening shades.

   ☐ Use household items that will darken windows, such as garbage bags or aluminum foil (use temporarily during sleep learning, then see if your child can sleep okay without them later).

   ☐ Install a night-light if you wish (though babies don't really need one, it may make it easier for you to see at night).

3. **Install white noise** (use temporarily during sleep learning; if houschold or neighborhood is busy, may need to continue using).

   ☐ Use an appliance (fan, humidifier, air purifier).

   ☐ Purchase sound machine with volume control (best for busier households or neighborhoods).

4. **Use footed blanket sleepers.**

Items I Need to Purchase
(such as white noise machine, darkening shade, or "Mommy Bear")

1. _____

2. _____

3. _____

4. _____

5. _____

6. _____

D. Review Sleep Aids

☐ Pacifier

- Stop reinserting unless your child is able to reinsert it on her own
100 percent of the time.

- If child can reinsert on own, place six or seven in crib so she can always find one.

☐ Stop using swaddle (after 4 months).

☐ Use music for wind-down only; make sure music is turned off when child goes down to sleep.

☐ Use a transitional object (small, safe blankie or animal).

E. My Child's Sleep Schedule

On this page, write down a goal schedule for your child's sleep and feeding.

Bedtime: _____

Wake time: _____

Nap 1: _____

Nap 2: _____

Nap 3: _____

(Fill in naps once you've planned your nap schedule in Chapter 5, "The Art of the Nap.")

F. My Child's Limit-Testing Behaviors

1. _____
   _____

2. _____
   _____

3. _____
   _____

4. _____
   _____

5. _____
   _____

For Verbal Children

☐ Make a personalized sleep book to help your child adjust to the changes you're making.

☐ Offer a "Mommy/Daddy Bear" so your child can cuddle with a transitional object as you gently set limits.

G. My Child's Weaning Schedule (for Nighttime Feeds)

	Time of First Feed _____ AM/PM	Time of Second Feed _____ AM/PM	Time of Third Feed _____ AM/PM
Night 1	___ oz. ___ min.	___ oz. ___ min.	___ oz. ___ min.
Night 2	___ oz. ___ min.	___ oz. ___ min.	___ oz. ___ min.
Night 3	___ oz. ___ min.	___ oz. ___ min.	___ oz. ___ min.
Night 4	___ oz. ___ min.	___ oz. ___ min.	___ oz. ___ min.
Night 5	___ oz. ___ min.	___ oz. ___ min.	___ oz. ___ min.
Night 6	___ oz. ___ min.	___ oz. ___ min.	___ oz. ___ min.

Sleep Planner: For Bed Sleepers

A. Bedtime Routine Checklist

Put a check next to the activities you would like to do each night. Then write a number next to each one so you can remember to do them in the same order every time.

____ ☐ Bath

____ ☐ Diaper or Pull-Ups (if appropriate) and pj's

____ ☐ Milk (if still drinking milk)

____ ☐ Quiet play on the floor (no stimulating toys)

____ ☐ Rocking

____ ☐ Story or books (including the one you make together about changes at bedtime)

____ ☐ Singing or music

____ ☐ Favorite ritual (such as saying good night to stuffed animals or the moon)

____ ☐ Turning on white noise

____ ☐ Offering blankie, "Mommy Bear," or other transitional object

____ ☐ Cuddling before leaving the room

____ ☐ Other:

_____

_____

_____

B. My Child's Sleep Associations

Write down the associations your child may have with falling asleep, such as sucking, motion, or lying down with a parent.

1. _____

2. _____

3. _____

4. _____

5. _____

C. Environmental Checklist

Use this checklist to get your child's sleeping space ready to begin sleep learning. If you don't have the environment quite right, *don't start sleep learning!* You want to give your child every possible chance to sleep well.

1. **Remove stimulating items from in and around the bed.**

   ☐ Toys

   ☐ Books

   ☐ Flashlights

   ☐ Other items: _____

   _____

   _____

2. **Make room dark** (on a scale of 10, if 10 is dark, go for 8 or 9!).

   ☐ Install room-darkening shades

☐ Use household items that will darken windows, such as garbage bags or aluminum foil (use temporarily during sleep learning, then see if your child can sleep okay without them later).

☐ Install a night-light

3. **Use footed blanket sleepers.**

4. **Install white noise** (use temporarily during sleep learning; if household or neighborhood is busy, may need to continue using).

☐ Use an appliance (fan, humidifier, air purifier)

☐ Purchase sound machine with volume control (best for busier households or neighborhoods).

5. **Safety proof the room** (pick up all toys, stools, or other items your child could trip over).

Items I Need to Purchase
(such as white noise machine, darkening shade, or "Mommy Bear")

1. _____

2. _____

3. _____

4. _____

5. _____

6. _____

D. Review Sleep Aids

☐ Pacifier (place six or seven in a bowl near the bed so he can always find one).

☐ Use music for wind-down only; make sure music is turned off when child goes down to sleep.

☐ Use a transitional object (lovey or stuffed animal).

E. My Child's Sleep Schedule

On this page, write down goal schedules for your child's sleep. The information on this page will not change as your child is learning how to sleep.

Bedtime: _____

Wake time: _____

Nap: _____

(Fill in naps once you've planned your nap schedule in Chapter 5, "The Art of the Nap.")

F. My Child's Limit-Testing Behaviors

1. _____

2. _____

3. _____

4. _____

5. _____

Things I Need to Prepare
(such as create special sleep book or safety-proof room)

1. _____

2. _____

3. _____

4. _____

APPENDIX B: Crying 911 (Emergency Help for Panicked Parents)

I n this appendix, we've included the most common questions we've heard from parents over the years, as well as the answers that we offer to parents we work with in our practice. Use this section once you've begun helping your child learn how to sleep through the night, when your child is crying and your confidence is wavering.

Q: Help! I want to give up!

A: You've just put your child down awake, and she is crying in protest. This may be the first time you haven't leapt to your baby's side as she cries, and every bone in your body is telling you to just pick her up and soothe her. If you have a toddler or older child, you may be listening to heartbreaking pleas for one more hug or to come lie down with him. But remember—these things are what you've already been doing for weeks, months, or years, and they haven't been helping your child sleep! If you go in and pick up your child or give in and lie down with him, you will calm him down temporarily, but you'll be right back where you started—with him dependent on you to go to sleep and thus waking throughout the night.

Q: I already tried letting my child cry, but it didn't work. How will using these methods be any different?

A: Many of the parents who contact us at Sleepy Planet tell us that they've tried letting their child "cry it out" to no avail. Once we discuss in detail what they tried, however, we can spot the fatal flaws that prevented their child from successfully learning how to sleep. These include any or all of the following:

- The parents simply shut the door and allowed their child to cry unassisted (not enough support for the child).

- They patted, hugged, or picked up their child during check-ins (too much interference, which serves as a tease and makes the crying go on much longer and harder).

- They allowed their child to cry for a certain length of time, then went in and picked her up (reinforcing the crying behavior).

- They sometimes allowed their child to cry, sometimes went in and fed him, and sometimes went in and patted his tummy (giving their child mixed messages).

- They allowed their child to cry for a night or two, then, not seeing perfect results, assumed the process wasn't working (needing more patience and perseverance).

- The *parents* couldn't stand the crying, so they stopped the process (needing to examine what the crying is bringing up for them).

- They failed to instill a consistent bedtime routine, put their child down too early or too late, or didn't create the right sleep environment.

Any of these common mistakes can prevent a child from learning how to sleep quickly. If you can spot the differences between what you've tried previously and what we're offering, then you know that there are a few adjustments to make to help your child sleep as well as she can.

Q: Will my child ever stop crying and fall asleep?

A: First and most important, your child *will stop crying* when going to sleep in the next couple of days. The crying *will not last forever!* You're allowing some crying, for a few minutes at a time, only in the interest of helping your child learn an important new skill. You can kiss her nonstop tomorrow. Remember, what's best for your child is getting the right sleep nutrition, so she'll grow and develop properly. You are doing the most important thing for her health and overall well-being: *supporting her need to sleep.*

If you have an older child, he cannot function well on too little sleep. He needs to sleep deeply without constant wakings or excursions around the house at night. He will be very proud of his accomplishments in the morning when you praise him, even if he's very mad at you right now. He also gets mad when you don't let him have ice cream before dinner, right? His protesting now is just like an "ice-cream tantrum." Hold your ground. It will be okay.

Q: How long will it take for my child to stop crying and fall asleep?

A: That depends a lot on you! Consistency is your number-one most important factor for success in this process. Most children cry less than an hour the first night going down—while supported with loving check-ins—and less each night thereafter. If your child cries a bit longer, don't panic. As long as you follow the guidelines in this book and remain consistent—*and* you're sure your child is not sick, teething, or in the middle of a developmental milestone—he will sleep soon.

If you consistently check in with your child at the same intervals each night and for naps, *and don't touch her or pick her up*, you will see progress very quickly. Most children are able to sleep well in less than five nights; naps may take a little longer, sometimes seven to ten days. With toddlers, or for children who have been used to being held while they sleep, the process sometimes takes a few days longer, though you should see significant progress after only a couple of days *if you stay consistent.*

Q: Do I have to do the check-ins if it just makes the crying worse?

A: If you find that checking in makes your child angrier when you leave again, try extending the interval for your check-ins by 5 to 15 minutes. If checking in still makes it worse at that point, follow your instincts: if it feels comfortable to you not to check in, experiment with leaving him be. Your child may then fall asleep very quickly.

Q: This is so hard. Isn't it easier to just go back to doing what we were doing?

A: We always urge moms and dads to try to look at the bigger picture when helping their child to sleep. What are the short-term benefits of allowing your child's old behavior to continue? You can certainly avoid the crying and frustration that comes with sleep learning. You don't have to put your life on hold while you allow your child to practice learning how to sleep. You can put your concerns about your child and your family's well-being on the back burner.

But what are the long-term effects of continuing to get poor sleep? How will you feel a couple of months or a year from now, when you are still waking several times a night and your child is demanding even more from you during the day? Will your marriage be able to sustain the lack of time together that all couples need to maintain a solid relationship during the child-rearing years? How would it impact your child if you were feeling chronically depressed, anxious, angry, or disconnected from your spouse? Finally, from a safety angle, if you continue to suffer from chronic sleep deprivation, will you be able to drive a car carefully, cook dinner without slicing into a finger or burning yourself, or have the strength to carry your child as he gets heavier? We think the answers are obvious, but they're sometimes difficult to see when you're already exhausted.

Q: I'm not sure I can do this, but I can't go back to what I was doing, either—what do I do now?

A: You're between a rock and a hard place: you know chronic sleep deprivation isn't good for your child, yet these first steps toward change are so difficult. But here's the good news: if you can get through these first few nights, you'll have accomplished the majority of your sleep learning! If you give up before you get there, though, your child will have cried for no reason, and that's not fair to any of you.

Remember, you are checking in frequently to reassure your child that you haven't left him, that you are calm and confident in his abilities, and that you love him. Helping him to sleep hasn't worked for any of you, so you are now helping him learn what he needs to do for himself.

Your child desperately needs her sleep. She won't feel happy or healthy without it. What's more, you and your spouse are also exhausted, and that is slowly causing damage to your relationship with each other and with the whole family. Your child is not getting the best of you if you are irritable and impatient, too tired to play, or yelling at each other.

Q: I can't help wondering, what is my child feeling or thinking right now?

A: If you are sleep learning with a baby, he is crying right now because he doesn't know—*yet*—how to put himself to sleep. If he could talk to you, he'd be saying, "What on earth do you guys think you're doing? You're out of your minds if you believe I can do this on my own. Get in here right now and rock me/feed me/fly me around the room like an airplane, or I'm going to keep throwing a huge fit!" He's frustrated because he's trying to learn an important new skill. But this certainly isn't the first or last time your child will feel frustration; frustration is a normal part of life.

You are a loving, caring, attentive, available parent, and right now you are allowing your child a few minutes and a little bit of space to learn how to fall asleep. Even though the first few nights are challenging, if you stay consistent and don't deviate from your plan, she will soon find something to do to soothe herself, like sucking her fingers or nuzzling her blankie, if she's a baby. Once she practices doing this a bunch of times, she will say to herself, "Aha! I get it now. I just do 'that thing,' and it's really relaxing! Who needs help? I'm hot stuff!"

If you have a toddler or preschooler, he is probably letting you know in no uncertain terms that you stink, or maybe he's giving you some version of, "I'll never, ever let you live this down!" But consider this: when you stop him from playing with the shiny kitchen knives, he's probably pretty mad then, too. Just because he's mad doesn't mean that he should be allowed to get what he wants. Stay loving when you check in; just talk to your child calmly and reassuringly. Then watch how he acts in the morning when you tell him how wonderful a job he did. He'll feel tremendously proud of his accomplishments.

Q: How am I ever going to get through this night?

A: Make yourself a promise: tonight, *just for one night*, you will follow your sleep plan to the letter and not deviate at all. You'll take a giant leap of faith and will follow the schedule you created in your Sleep Planner and follow all of the guidelines we've outlined for your child's age range *consistently*. Then, if you're miserable in the morning, you can trash the whole thing and burn our book. We won't take it personally! But we're betting that it won't come to that, because even though your first night won't be the most fun you've ever had as a mom and a dad, you'll find that your child eventually does learn how to put herself to sleep. Finally. We promise—this learning process will go remarkably quickly if you stick to the plan. Take this in bite-size chunks. Don't think about tomorrow yet. Just think about getting through tonight—and remember that after you get through tonight, you've done a great deal of the hardest work already.

If the crying is really getting to you, ask your spouse to do some check-ins while you take a walk around the block. Sometimes putting on a little music or turning down the monitor helps to make the time go a bit faster. Take some deep breaths to help you calm down: breathe in to the count of five, then try to imagine how you'll feel when your child falls asleep. Imagine saying to yourself, "Oh my gosh! He actually did it!" Can you feel even just a hint of that possibility? Can you imagine how excited you'll be?

Q: How can I face my child when I feel like I'm letting him down?

A: Once you've made the decision to begin sleep learning, try to stay as positive as you can. Kids sense anxiety, and if you're white-knuckling your way through this process, she'll feel anxious, too (and have a harder time relaxing into sleep). When you do a check-in, use your best Oscar-caliber acting techniques and sound as calm and confident as you can. Tell her you know she can do it. Then, when you come back out to your sleep station, cry if you need to. Eat that entire carton of ice cream. It's okay to feel sad and anxious as both you and your child are struggling. Be gentle with yourself, and take your time. Then try to calm down before you go in again.

Remember, you are not hurting your child by setting some limits around sleeping. There is absolutely no evidence that allowing a baby or young child to experience a small amount of frustration causes long-term damage. And also remember, you will continue to give your child as much love and attention during the day, or between sleep periods, as you always have. Once sleep learning is over—it usually lasts about a week altogether—you won't have to listen to any crying at bedtime anymore. Imagine your child going to sleep without tears *or* protest . . . that dream will be a reality soon!

Q: I don't think I can manage to hear my child cry at night and then during the day for naps, too. Can I work on just the nights first?

Normally, we do encourage families to work on both nighttime and daytime sleep simultaneously, so that your child can practice new skills round the clock and so that you can move beyond sleep learning quickly and enjoy plenty of good rest. However, if you're extremely sensitive to your child's crying, you can postpone working on daytime sleep. The brain actually organizes night sleep and day sleep separately, so you can follow the steps outlined in this book to help your child to sleep more independently at night but continue to assist him in getting to sleep during the day. If you do wait to work on naps, try to get your child to sleep without helping him directly, such as by strolling or driving him rather than feeding, rocking, or bouncing. This way, he'll be less dependent on you, and will learn to nap well more quickly when you're ready to teach him. If driving or strolling doesn't work or aren't an option for you, just continue to do whatever you've typically done to help him sleep during the day. Although it may take a bit longer to solidify nighttime sleep without the daytime practice, your child will still learn how to sleep well at night.

Do be careful, though, to make sure your child gets enough daytime sleep, however you help her do that, so that she's not overtired by the time she goes to sleep at night. If she's overtired going down at bedtime, the cortisol in her body will cause disrupted sleep (for more on cortisol, see "Sleep Stealer #5" in Chapter 2).

APPENDIX C: Sleep Chart

Use this chart to track your child's progress while she learns to sleep. (Alternatively, you can download a chart from the "Tips & Tools" section of our website, www.sleepy-planet.com.) On the first night you start, write down the date and what time you put your child down to sleep. Then, record each check-in time and tally up the total amount of time she took to fall asleep. If she wakes in the night, record the wake-up time and your check-in times the same way. For naps, track your progress on the second chart.

Sleep Chart

NIGHTS

Date	Bedtime or Waking	1st Check	2nd Check	3rd Check	4th Check	5th Check	6th Check	Total Time

NAPS

Date	Naptime	1st Check	2nd Check	3rd Check	4th Check	5th Check	6th Check	Total Time

APPENDIX D: Average Sleep Needs by Age

Please note that the ranges and totals given below are approximate, and that some children need less sleep while others need more. When helping your child learn how to sleep, you'll want to shoot for the minimum of 11 hours at night and 1 hour for each nap. Paying attention to your child's mood and behavior is the best gauge of whether your child is getting the right amount of sleep.

AGE	NIGHTTIME	NAPS	TOTAL HOURS
Newborn	Unpredictable/ varies widely	Unpredictable/ varies widely	Unpredictable/ varies widely
4 months	11–12 hours	3–4 hours *(made up in three or four naps)*	14 to 16 hours
6 months	11–12 hours	2–3¼ hours *(made up in two or three naps)*	13 to 15¼ hours
9 months	11–12 hours	2–3 hours *(made up in two naps)*	13 to 15 hours
12 months	11–12 hours	1½–3 hours *(made up in one or two naps)*	12½ to 15 hours

AGE	NIGHTTIME	NAPS	TOTAL HOURS
18 months	11 hours	1½–3 hours *(usually one nap)*	12½ to 14 hours
2 years	11 hours	1½–3 hours *(one nap)*	12½ to 14 hours
3 years	11–12 hours*	Up to 2 hours *(maybe no nap)*	11 to 14 hours
4 years	11–12 hours	Up to 2 hours *(maybe no nap)*	11 to 12 hours
5 years	11–12 hours	No nap	11 to 12 hours

Children may sleep longer at night after they drop their nap.

Organizations and Websites

American Academy of Pediatrics
www.AAP.org

Babycenter
www.Babycenter.com

La Leche League International
www.lalecheleague.org

Modern Mom
www.modernmom.com

National Organization of Mothers of Twins Clubs (NOMOTC)
www.nomotc.com

National Sleep Foundation
www.sleepfoundation.org

Postpartum Support International
www.postpartum.net

SIDS Alliance
www.sidsalliance.com

Products
(white noise machines, safety railings, safety gates, crib tents, bedding, etc.)

Babies R Us
www.babiesrus.com

One Step Ahead
www.onestepahead.com

The Pump Station
www.pumpstation.com

Radio Shack
www.radioshack.com

The Right Start
www.Rightstart.com

Parenting Books

On Babies

A Mother's Circle *Jean Kunhardt and Lisa Spiegel*
A must-have, easy-to-read, comprehensive book for both mom and dad on the transition to parenthood. Can be ordered online at www.sohoparentingcenter.com.

Caring for Your Baby and Young Child *Steven Shelov, M.D.*
Comprehensive encyclopedia for health, illness, and safety.

Child of Mine: Feeding with Love and Good Sense *Ellyn Satter*
Nutrition and feeding guide for both infants and toddlers.

The Experts' Guide to the Baby Years *Created by Samantha Ettus*
Top parenting experts offer advice on everything from breast-feeding to baby-proofing.

The Happiest Baby on the Block *Harvey Karp, M.D.*
Whether you choose the book or the DVD, Dr. Karp's methods offer parents a variety of techniques to soothe fussy newborns. Good for helping children under 4 months get to sleep.

The Modern Girl's Guide to Motherhood *Jane Buckingham*
A fresh take on navigating the first years of parenthood, offered with intelligence and humor.

Touchpoints *T. Berry Brazelton*
An essential reference book for your child's emotional and behavioral development.

Your One-Year-Old *Louise Bates Ames, Ph.D.*
This condensed book guides you through the developmental issues that parents face during the first year. Series includes books for other ages.

Your Self-Confident Baby *Magda Gerber and Allison Johnson*
Fascinating information about respect in parenting; great for first year.

On Toddlers

1-2-3 . . . The Toddler Years *Irene Van der Zande*
Includes information on development, communication, and discipline for 1- to 3-year-olds.

Becoming the Parent You Want to Be *Laura Davis and Janis Keyser*
A sourcebook of strategies for the first five years in relation to both parent and child development.

The Blessing of a Skinned Knee *Wendy Mogel*
An inspirational book that teaches how children can use challenges to build good coping skills and competence.

Love and Logic Magic in Early Childhood *Jim Fay and Charles Fay, Ph.D.*
Practical, easy-to-use book on using positive discipline with young children, while encouraging respect, responsibility, and self-worth of the child.

The Challenging Child *Stanley Greenspan, M.D.*
A look at personality types and the challenges they present.

The Difficult Child *Stanley Turecki*
Details how to help and cope with a temperamentally difficult child.

How to Behave So Your Preschooler Will Too *Sal Severe*
Wonderful and positive book on limit setting and discipline.

How to Talk So Kids Will Listen & Listen So Kids Will Talk
Adele Faber and Elaine Mazlish
Essentials of communication between parents and children.

Parent School *Jerry and Lorin Biederman*
A compilation of important insights from two leading parenting experts. Absolutely inspirational!

The Wonder of Boys and the Wonder of Girls *Michael Gurian*
A look at psychosexual development and how it pertains to personality and parenting.

Your Two-Year-Old *Louise Bates Ames, Ph.D.*
Concise but comprehensive information on your child's development. See also other books in series for children of different ages.

On Second-Time Parenting

Welcoming Your Second Baby *Vicky Lansky*
Excellent handbook of helpful tips and advice for a smooth transition
for parents and siblings.

Siblings without Rivalry *Adele Faber and Eileen Mazlish*
Helping siblings to interact in positive ways.

Books for Young Children

Sleep

Good Night Moon *Margaret Wise Brown*

Good Night Gorilla *Peggy Rathmann*

Bedtime for Frances *Russell Hoban*

The Napping House *Audrey Wood*

Time for Bed *Mem Fox*

I Am Not Sleepy and I Will Not Go to Bed *Lauren Child*

Behavior and Feelings

The Chocolate-Covered-Cookie Tantrum *Deborah Blumenthal*

Mama, Do You Love Me? *Barbara M. Joose*

No Biting *Karen Katzs*

Hands Are Not for Hitting *Martine Agassi*

The Kissing Hand *Audrey Penn*

Today I Feel Silly *Jamie Lee Curtis*

When Sophie Gets Angry *Molly Garrett Bang*

The Way I Feel books *Cornelia Maude Spelman*
Sad, Jealous, and Scared—best for older toddler.

Other

Best Word Book Ever *Richard Scarry*

Cars and Trucks and Things That Go *Richard Scarry*

Once Upon a Potty *Alona Frankel*
Separate books for girls and boys.

REFERENCES

Carpenter, R. G., L. M. Irgens, P. S. Blair, P. D. England, P. Fleming, J. Huber, G. Jorch, and P. Schreuder, "Sudden unexplained infant death in 20 regions in Europe: case control study." *The Lancet* 363 (Jan. 17, 2004).

Gais, S., W. Plihal, U. Wagner, and J. Born, "Early Sleep Triggers Memory for Early Visual Discrimination Skills," *Nature Neuroscience* 3 (2000): 1335–9.

National Institutes of Health website, "For Parents: Why Sleep Is Important," *www.nhlbi.nih.gov*).

Pollock, J. I., "Predictors and long-term associations of reported sleep difficulties in infancy." *Journal of Reproductive and Infant Psychology* 10 (1992): 151–168.

Richman, N., J. E. Stevenson, and P. J. Graham, "Behavior problems in three-year-old children: An epidemiological study in a London bourough." *Journal of Child Psychology and Psychiatry* 12 (1975): 5–33.

Sadeh, A., R. Gruber, and A. Raviv, "Sleep, Neurobehavioral Functioning, and Behavior Problems in School-Age Children," *Child Development* 73 (2002): 405–17.

INDEX

A

acute teething, 144–145, 234–235

B

bed, transition from crib to, 178–179, 184, 199, 209–212

bed buddy, 211

bed sleepers

  alternate sleep learning tips, 113–114

  checking in, 62–64, 104–105

  early-morning wakings, 71

  napping practice for, 100–101

  night wakings, 69

  proper sleeping environment, 22–23

  transitioning from your bed to child's, 208–209

bedroom, desensitizing child to, 190

bedtime, choosing and enforcing, 29–31

bedtime routine

  inconsistencies in, 16–18

  language development and, 167

  making sure child stays awake, 56–57, 120–121, 129–130

  moving and, 231, 232

  napping and, 102–105, 160

  for newborns, 128–129, 130

  separation anxiety and, 143

  sleep resistance and, 170

  in transition from crib to bed, 211–212

  travel and, 227–228

  for verbal children, 18

blankets, safety tips, 27

blankies. *See* transitional objects

books

  to deal with fears, 191

  to prepare for transitions, 184–188, 197

  for separation anxiety, 195

bottle-feeding

  night feeding and, 39

  weaning from, 163–164

  weaning from night feeding, 45–48

breast-feeding

  caffeine and, 45

  night feedings and, 39, 40–42

  weaning from night feedings, 40–45

C

caffeine, breast-feeding and, 45

caregivers

  napping and, 220

  support for sleep plan by, 14–15, 220

checking in, 60

  after vomiting, 206

  alternate approach, 112–113

  bed sleepers, 62–64

  cheating, 62

  cosleeping and, 117

  crib sleepers, 60–62

  early-morning wakings, 70–71

  extending, 63

  naps and, 103–105

  night wakings, 68–69

  tag-team approach, 63

children

  caving in to demands by, 181–183

children *(cont'd)*
  choices offered to, 36, 58,
     159–160, 181–184
  curiosity in, 177
  decision-making in, 177
  emotional changes in, 174
  fears in, 189–191
  hours of sleep needed by, 29–30,
     134–135, 269–270
  imagination in, 189
  overtiredness in, 29, 86–87, 194,
     238
  preempting requests after bed-
     time, 37
  sleep deprivation and, 7–9, 79
  stress in, 192, 194
  tiredness (sleep readiness) signs,
     28
  verbally developed, 18, 56, 57,
     71, 82–83, 101, 244
choices, offering to children, 36, 58,
     159–160, 181–184
chronic teething, 144
clothing, for sleeping, 24
cognitive skills, sleep resistance and
     learning, 159
colic, 204–205
consistency, importance of, 16–18,
     80, 83
cortisol, 28–29, 137, 163
cosleeping, 114–116
  early-morning wakings and, 117
  middle-of-the-road option,
     116–117
  parents' intimate time and, 118
  safe sleeping environment,
     118–119
  SIDS and, 116, 127
  transitioning from your bed to
     child's, 208–209

weaning night feedings, 119
crawling, sleep learning and, 139,
     235–236
crib sleepers
  alternate sleep learning tips,
     112–113
  checking in, 60–62, 103
  children under three, 199
  climbing out of crib, 236–237
  early-morning wakings, 70
  napping practice, 100–101
  night wakings, 68
  proper sleeping environment,
     22–23
  safety-proofing the crib, 148
  transitioning to bed, 178–179,
     184, 199, 209–212, 237
crib tent, 237
crying, 59
  developmental milestones and, 81
  emergency help with, 259–266
  holding while, 65
  at nap time, 239–240
  parents' reaction to, 65, 80–81
  reducing during check-ins, 61,
     104
  reduction as sign that child is
     learning, 63
  safety of allowing, 79–81, 112
  sleep learning and, 75–78,
     237–238
  vomiting with, 205–206
  See also protesting
curiosity, 177

D
"Daddy Bear," 211
"Daddy Book," 168–169
darkness, required for sleeping,
     23–24

day care providers. *See* caregivers
daylight savings time, sleep learning
    and, 228–230
decision-making, in children, 177
demands, allowing in children,
    181–183
developmental milestones, 13–14
    newborns, 124–126, 127–130
    4 to 6 months, 138–139
    9 to 12 months, 147, 148–149
    12 to 18 months, 154–156
    18 to 24 months, 165–167
    2 to 3 years, 175–178
    3 to 5 years, 180–188
    crying and, 81
    early waking and, 243–244
    limit testing and, 31
    motor skills, 140–141
    sleep disruption solutions, 149–150
    sleep learning and, 13–14,
        235–236
distractibility, during feedings, 138
dream catchers, 192
dream feeds, 13, 39, 49

E

early morning wakings, 69–71, 117,
    120, 162–163, 230, 235,
    242–243
"Energizer Bunny syndrome,"
    158–160
extinction burst, 236

F

family systems theory, 4–5
fears, 24, 184, 189–191
    desensitizing and calming, 190–191
feeding
    distractibility during, 138
    and nap schedule, 240

solid foods, 146–147
    See also night feeding

H

Happiest Baby on the Block, The
    (Karp), 125–126
hunger
    early morning waking and, 244
    night feedings and, 66

I

illness, sleep learning and, 233–234
individuation, 142, 155–156
intermittent reinforcement, 80

K

Karp, Dr. Harvey, 125–126

L

limit setting, 183
limit testing, 155–157, 166, 173,
    177–178, 200–201
lovies. *See* transitional objects

M

marriage, sleep deprivation and, 3–5
"Mommy Bear," 27, 36, 195, 211
"Mommy Book," 162, 168–169
"monster spray," 191
motor skills, development of, 176
moving, sleep learning and, 230–232
music, as sleep aid, 26

N

napping, 30, 85–86
    4- to 6-month olds, 88–91,
        136–137
    6- to 9-month-olds, 91–93, 140
    9- to 12-month olds, 93–94,
        147–148, 148–159
    12- to 24-month-olds, 95–98,
        152, 163

napping (*cont'd*)
    2- to 3-year-olds, 98–99, 175
    3- to 5-year-olds, 179–180
    bedtime routine for, 16, 17,
        102–105
    caregiver and, 220
    cat naps, 108
    check-ins, 103–105
    cortisol and, 137, 163
    crying when put down for,
        239–240
    daylight savings time and,
        229–230
    daytime wake windows, 87, 95
    emergency naps, 109
    keeping child awake, 102, 103,
        238
    learning time, 108
    in motion, 160, 239
    pendulum behavior, 106–107
    pooping and, 207–208
    poor timing of, 86
    practice time for, 100–101
    praising your child, 105
    problems with, 86–87
    procrastinating, 107
    reminding verbal children about
        changes, 101
    resistance to, 157
    scheduled feedings and, 240
    separating from nighttime sleep
        learning, 108–109
    sleep station for, 101
    starting too late, 96
    step-by-step sleep for, 100–106
    timing of, 238–239
    transitioning from three naps to
        two, 92–93, 239
    transitioning from two naps to
        one, 96–98, 152
    traveling and, 226, 227
newborns, sleep needs of, 124–126,
    127–130, 269
night feeding, 13, 38–39
    babies over 12 months, 40, 162
    babies under 12 months, 39–40
    commonly asked questions, 48–51
    early morning mixed messages, 49
    hunger and, 66
    pacing, 42–45
    waking up before feeding time, 67
    weaning from, 40–48, 67, 119,
        121, 234
    See also feeding
night-lights, 24, 190
night terrors, 193–194
night wakings, 19–20, 68
    bed sleepers, 69
    crib sleepers, 68
    extinction burst and, 236
    in toddlers, 162–163
nightmares, 191–192

O
object permanence, 161, 166
overstimulation, 128
overtiredness, 29, 86–87, 194, 238

P
pacifiers
    SIDS prevention and, 25
    as sleep aid, 26
    weaning from, 163–164
pain relievers, 145
parallel play, 177
parents
    adjusting to a newborn, 133–134
    concerns over child's crying,
        75–76
    coping with exhaustion, 131–132

postpartum depression, 133
reactions to child's crying, 65,
   80–81
reducing tension while child
   cries, 65
separating own feelings from
   child's, 183
single and sleep learning,
   221–222
sleep deprivation and, 5–7, 79,
   155
sleeping in child's room,
   113–114, 212–213
working
   bedtime routine, 17
   return to work and sleep plan,
      15, 218–219
partial arousals (awakenings), 19–20
peek-a-boo games, 142
permissiveness, 182–183
photo album, for separation anxiety,
   195
"Pick Me Up/Put Me Down
   Syndrome," 154–155
plane trips, 223–224
plateaus, 73
pooping, sleep learning and,
   207–208
postpartum depression, 133
potty training, 171
   child's interest in, 177
   nighttime issues and solutions,
      200–201
   as transition, 184, 200–201
protesting, 61
   early-morning wakings, 71
   at nap time, 94, 104, 106
   in older children, 82–83
   reduction of, 64, 105
   time consumed by, 65

in toddlers and preschoolers, 184
   See also crying

R
reflux, 204–205
room temperature, 23

S
safety gates, 36–37, 56, 62, 69, 71,
   104
   alternative to, 38, 63–64, 69, 71,
      104–105
school, anxiety about, 196–197
self-regulation skills, 181
self-soothing, 78, 82, 120, 127, 206
separation anxiety, 31, 112–113, 184
   at 9 to 12 months, 149, 150
   at 12 to 18 months, 161–163
   at 18 to 24 months, 166, 167
   at 2 to 3 years, 194
   sleep disruption and, 168–169
   sneaking out and, 195
shadow play, 190
siblings
   birth of, 184, 197–199
   sleep learning for, 216–218,
      240–242
SIDS. See sudden infant death syndrome (SIDS)
sleep aids, 25–28
sleep associations, 19–22, 25
sleep book, personalized, 32–35, 57,
   121
Sleep Chart, 56, 60, 267–268
sleep cues, 17
sleep deprivation, 1, 2–9, 79, 155,
   240
sleep learning
   alternate methods, 111–114
   crying and, 75–78

sleep learning (*cont'd*)
  day care and, 221
  daylight savings time and,
      228–230
  developmental milestones and,
      13–14, 235–236
  family schedule and, 14
  illness and, 12–13, 233–234
  language development and, 167
  moving and, 230–232
  in newborns, 127–128
  proper weight to start, 13, 125,
      137
  separation anxiety and, 195
  for siblings, 216–218, 240–242
  single parents and, 221–222
  teething and, 12
  transitions and, 201
  for twins (multiple births),
      214–216
  weaning from bottle, pacifier, or
      blankie, 164
  for working parents, 218–219
sleep needs, 29–30, 134–135,
      269–270
  in newborns, 124–126
  4 to 6 months, 135–139
  6 to 9 months, 139–140
  9 to 12 months, 147–148
  12 to 18 months, 153–154
  18 to 24 months, 165
  2 to 3 years, 175
  3 to 5 years, 179–180
sleep plan, 11–12
  after first night, 71–72
  bedtime routine, 56–57
  beginning, 54
  creating sleep station, 55
  customizing, 15–16
  falling asleep, 66

  night wakings, 68–71
  plateaus, 73
  putting child to bed awake, 58,
      120–121, 129–130
  readiness and preparation, 12–15
  reviewing, 51
  sleep stealers, 16–38
  verbal child preparation, 56
Sleep Planner, 56, 215, 247–257
sleep readiness signs, 28
sleep resistance
  Energizer Bunny syndrome,
      158–160
  naps, 157, 158–160, 169–170
  nighttime, 157, 169–170
  stimulation and, 170
Sleep Rules, 73, 198–199
sleep station, 55, 66, 68, 101
sleep stealers
  inconsistent bedtime routine,
      16–18, 80
  limit testing, 31–38, 155–157,
      166, 173, 177–178
  mistimed sleep schedule, 28–31
  misuse of sleep aids, 25–28
  night eating, 38–48
  parent's presence required to fall
      asleep, 19–22
  poor sleep environment, 22–25
sleep windows, 28
sleepwalking, 193–194
smoking, 119
solid foods, starting, 146–147
sticker charts, 73
stimulation, at bedtime, 170
stress
  night terrors and, 194
  nightmares and, 192
sudden infant death syndrome
      (SIDS)

cosleeping and, 116
pacifiers and, 25
prevention of, 126–127
smoking and, 119
swaddling, as sleep aid, 26

T
tantrums, 32, 82, 113, 180
See also crying; protesting
teething, 144–145
sleep learning and, 12, 234–235
time zone changes, 225–227
transitional objects
separation anxiety and, 143, 195
as sleep aids, 27–28, 163, 191, 232
transitional objects *(cont'd)*
weaning from, 163–164
transitions
birth of sibling, 184, 197–199
books to prepare child for, 184–188
from crib to bed, 178–179
potty training, 184, 200–201
preparing toddlers for, 170
sleep and, 201
starting school, 196–197
in toddlers and preschoolers, 184

from your bed to child's bed, 208–209
traveling, 222–223
bedtime routine and, 227–228
creating proper sleep environment when, 225
time zone changes, 225–227
trip logistics, 223–224
twins (multiple births), sleep learning for, 213–216

V
"vacation schedule," 226
verbal skills development
18-24 months, 167
2 to 3 years, 176
vomiting, 205–206

W
wake time, choosing, 29–30
wake windows, daytime, 87, 95
waking
early-morning, 69–70, 117, 163, 242–244
at night, 19–20, 68–69, 162–163
a sleeping child, 216
weaning. See night feeding
weight, sleep plan and, 13, 125, 137
white noise, 24, 25, 214, 215, 225, 243

ABOUT THE AUTHORS

As cofounders of Sleepy Planet, Jennifer Waldburger and Jill Spivack are recognized experts in both sleep and parent education. They have been featured in a variety of media, including *The Wall Street Journal*, *CBS Evening News*, *Inside Edition*, *Variety*, *Fit Pregnancy*, *Los Angeles Children*, *Los Angeles*, Fit TV's *Guru to Go*, *City Baby LA*, and *Los Angeles Daily News*. They are also the resident sleep experts on ModernMom.com.

Jill Spivack, LMSW, completed her graduate studies at University of Southern California and worked as a psychotherapist at Cedars-Sinai Medical Center's Early Childhood Department. Her involvement in pediatric sleep began in 1997, when Ms. Spivack was a typically overtired mother of an 8-month-old who had trouble sleeping through the night. Desperate for sleep but anxious about hearing her baby cry, Jill, who was then residing in New York City, turned to a local parenting center for help. When both her son and the whole family began sleeping soundly a few nights later, she realized what a valuable service she had received. She began working shortly thereafter at the Soho Parenting Center in New York as a parent educator, psychotherapist, and sleep consultant. After relocating to Los Angeles in 1999, she cofounded Childsleep and then went on to cofound Sleepy Planet.

Jennifer Waldburger, LCSW, began her professional career as a writer and editor in New York City, working for such publications as *Town & Country* magazine, *Redbook, Good Housekeeping*, and *Harper's Bazaar*. She earned her master's degree in social work at the University of Wisconsin, Madison. As a practicing psychotherapist, Jennifer noticed that many families were severely sleep deprived and functioning poorly due to exhaustion. She then cofounded The Sleeping Child, a pediatric sleep consultation business, in Chicago in 2001. She joined Childsleep as co-owner in 2003, and cofounded Sleepy Planet in 2006, where she offers private sleep consultations and parent education for parents of young children and leads new-mother groups. Jennifer also maintains a private psychotherapy practice in Los Angeles, California. In addition, Jennifer does healing and energy work with families, particularly parents and young children.

www.sleepyplanet.com

For more great tips and products to help
your child sleep – including audio
CDs and DVDs – please visit:

www.thesleepeasysolution.com

"With compassion and expertise, Sleepy Planet targets your
child's specific sleep needs and supports parents through
the emotional side of sleep learning. I highly recommend
these methods as both a pediatrician and a mother."

— Sonya Gohill, MD, Pediatrician